KU-442-790

AS Economics
UNIT 3
2ND EDITION

Module 2883: The National and International Economy

John Hearn

Philip Allan Updates
Market Place
Deddington
Oxfordshire
OX15 0SE

tel: 01869 338652
fax: 01869 337590
e-mail: sales@philipallan.co.uk
www.philipallan.co.uk

ISBN-13: 978-0-86003-930-3
ISBN-10: 0-86003-930-7

This Guide has been written specifically to support students preparing for the OCR AS Economics Unit 3 examination. The content has been neither approved nor endorsed by OCR and remains the sole responsibility of the author.

Printed by Information Press, Eynsham, Oxford

Environmental information
The paper on which this title is printed is sourced from managed, sustainable forests.

AS Economics

Contents

Introduction

■ ■ ■

Content Guidance

■ ■ ■

Questions and Answers

Introduction

'The National and International Economy' (Module 2883) is one of three compulsory modules you will study in order to complete the AS specification in economics. It is probably the third module you have studied in the first year of A-levels after 'The Market System' (Module 2881) and 'Market Failure and Government Intervention' (Module 2882). Of the three modules listed above, 'The National and International Economy' is the most heavily weighted in terms of the mark allocation to the final result. It accounts for 40% of the total AS mark and 20% of the A-level mark. It is also an important foundation for the final compulsory A2 module 'Economics in a European Context' (2888).

An understanding of governments' macroeconomic objectives and the techniques used to reach the targets are important in this module. When establishing policy, forecasting plays an important part in decision-making, so students need to be aware of the strengths and weaknesses of both creating and using forecasts. Remember that forecasts are not facts — there are no facts about the future.

Throughout this module, the most important model you must learn to use is the aggregate supply/aggregate demand (AS/AD) model. It can be used to illustrate what may happen to the economy when either demand-side or supply-side policies are employed in macroeconomic management.

As soon as possible, students need to familiarise themselves with statistics and forecasts similar to those that are likely to be used in the examination. The internet provides a range of websites from which information can be gathered. Any search engine from an internet service provider can be a useful starting point. For example, type in 'inflation' or 'unemployment' and follow the options that are made available on-screen. Some useful websites are listed below:

- www.statistics.gov.uk
- www.bankofengland.co.uk
- www.hm-treasury.gov.uk/press
- www.ecb.int (European Central Bank)
- www.worldbank.org (for worldwide data and maps)
- www.census.gov/main/www/stat_int.html (a list of international agencies that provide statistics)
- www.un.org (and follow the links through 'text version' to 'Cyber School Bus' and 'Infonation' among a choice of other useful sites)

How to use this guide

This introduction explains what the examining board is looking for and the skills required to achieve those targets. It will also remind you that your revision plan should not start when the course is finished, but should be prepared and planned from the very first lesson.

The second part of the unit guide — Content Guidance — offers an overview of 'The National and International Economy' and its four main areas of study:

- government macroeconomic policy objectives and indicators of national economic performance
- aggregate demand and aggregate supply: the determinants of output, employment and prices
- the application of macroeconomic policy instruments
- structure and essential determinants of international transactions

For each study area, there is a clear statement regarding the skills that must be developed. By the time of the examination, you must have learnt the definitions of a number of key words, and be able to understand certain concepts, hypotheses and theories. However, understanding is not enough, and the Content Guidance section also highlights the things you need to be able to explain, analyse, apply and evaluate in the way required for the award of a high grade.

The third part of the guide — Questions and Answers — includes six mock examinations which are subdivided into the case study and questions, followed by a mark scheme and two answers to grade A and grade C standards. The best way to use this section is as part of an intensive revision programme towards the end of the course. The reason for this is that each case study includes a range of questions that are spread across the whole specification and it would be counter-productive to test yourself on things you have not yet learnt. Below is a list of recommendations for using the case study questions and answers.

(1) During the early stages of the course, it may be useful to read through the questions only, without reference to the case study itself. This will provide a focus for the work you are doing and help you identify the things you will need to master before you can sit the examination with confidence.

(2) Towards the end of the course, find time to complete one or two case studies unseen, but also untimed. Then use the mark scheme to guide you through marking your own script. This is a useful exercise because giving yourself the examiner's job can focus your attention on what is and what is not important. It is quality and not quantity that counts. A rough guide to the marks associated with each grade is as follows:

Grade A	80%+
Grade B	70–79%
Grade C	60–69%
Grade D	50–59%
Grade E	40–49%

Once you have marked your own answers, compare them with the grade A and grade C answers.

(3) At the end of the course — or with approximately 1 month to go before the examination — plan to intersperse the remaining four questions into your final revision programme. This time, observe strictly the examination timings so that you familiarise yourself with how much can be achieved in 1 hour. Be guided in the time you spend on the questions by the mark allocation at the end of each question and its subdivisions (e.g. if there are 60 minutes in which to achieve 45 marks, each mark is worth 1 minute 20 seconds of your precious time).

On the examination paper it is worth counting down, say, 24 marks on the paper and marking it with '32' so that you have a guide to how much of the examination should be completed after 32 minutes.

(4) When you look through the grade A and grade C answers, read carefully any comments that appear after the mark given to each sub-question. These comments offer useful hints and will help you avoid the all-too-common mistakes made by the unprepared examination candidate.

Assessment objectives

Two broad skills are being assessed, which can be divided into:
- understanding
- expression

Assessment objectives	Skills	Percentage of total mark
Level 1	The ability to understand and express knowledge of the specification content, e.g. know that the government's macroeconomic objectives are a high level of employment, a sustained low rate of inflation, a satisfactory balance on external account and economic growth.	30%
Level 2	The ability to apply knowledge and understanding critically to the problems and issues that manifest themselves, e.g. understand the economic implications of high unemployment, accelerating inflation, balance of payments disequilibrium and negative economic growth.	30%
Level 3	The ability to use economic principles to analyse the problems and issues, e.g. use the AS/AD model to illustrate and analyse the main macro-economic problems.	20%
Level 4	The ability to reflect upon economic arguments, evaluate evidence and make informed judgements as an economist, e.g. does solving one macro-economic problem create conflicts with the policies used to solve the other problems, and if so how are the resulting trade-offs evaluated?	20%

Understanding

In some examinations, it has been possible for students to show an understanding of a subject and achieve a good mark on, say, a multiple-choice question paper but not be able to express that understanding clearly. Consequently, they achieve a relatively low mark on an essay paper. In this examination, however, there are no separate papers so you need to understand the subject and choose your words, numbers, formulae and diagrams carefully when answering the questions because this will determine your final mark. In addition to this, you are informed that one question will require you to write in continuous prose, and a proportion of the marks allocated to this question will test your ability to organise your thoughts and express them, using a form of writing that is appropriate to the question. Sentences must be legible with correct spelling, grammar and punctuation. This means that, if at the end of the examination you have time to check only one thing, make sure it is your answer to this last question.

Expression

The examining board separates the assessment objectives into four skill levels. These are illustrated in the table on page 6 by reference to the government's macro-economic objectives.

It is important to note that the assessment objectives for AS are weighted more heavily towards Levels 1 and 2, while the A2 papers that complete the A-level specification show a 30% weighting to Levels 3 and 4 and a 20% weighting to Levels 1 and 2.

Planning your work and preparing a revision strategy

- Get hold of a copy of the specification and plan a structure into which to fit your notes.
- Make sure you compile notes on the whole specification. Do not leave any gaps because all questions in the examination are compulsory. It is therefore not possible to be selective without taking unnecessary risks.
- When you take notes from relevant material, try and put them into your own words. This process helps to develop and organise thoughts and is therefore much more useful than just copying your notes verbatim.
- Summarise when taking notes and use a highlighter pen to emphasise key points and help focus your attention.
- Always ask yourself if your notes will make sense in 3 months' time.
- Whenever a planned or unplanned opportunity arises to practise the higher level skills, take it — even if it means talking to yourself or arguing with other members of the family.
- In the examination, the requirement to use higher-level skills in your answer will usually be indicated in the question by the following words:

Analyse...	Examine...
Elucidate...	Explain why...

while evaluation will be indicated by:

Evaluate...	To what extent...?
Discuss...	Do you agree...?
Comment...	

- As early as possible, identify the dates of your examination(s) so that you can prepare a revision strategy. You should include a portion of time that can be used if any emergency should arise.
- Avoid the tendency to revise the material you already know and ignore the more difficult parts of the course. It is reasonable to assume that the aspects you find difficult are going to appear in the examination as a test of higher-level skills.
- The process of organisation, preparation and revision that goes on throughout the year will have rooted some content firmly in your long-term memory. Over the last few weeks, help your short-term memory to upload the final details by using acronyms to remember lists, patterns to remember links, and key words to trigger a series of associated points.

Useful references

The main textbook for this module and the AS is *Economics for AS* edited by Colin Bamford and published by Cambridge University Press.

The *AS/A-Level Economics Essential Word Dictionary* by John Hearn, published by Philip Allan Updates, includes all the important definitions and terms referred to in module specifications.

The *AS/A-Level Economics Exam Revision Notes* by John Hearn, published by Philip Allan Updates, covers the basic economic theory used throughout the A-level course. Pages 84–123 cover the theory needed for 'The National and International Economy' module.

Content
Guidance

This section of the guide outlines the topic areas of Module 3 which are as follows:
- Government macroeconomic policy objectives and indicators of national economic performance
- Aggregate demand and aggregate supply: the determinants of output, employment and prices
- The application of macroeconomic policy instruments
- Structure and essential determinants of international transactions

Government macroeconomic policy objectives and indicators of national economic performance

The balance of supply and demand at the aggregate level would ideally produce full employment, stability in the average level of prices, equilibrium on the balance of payments and sustainable economic growth. These are the government's macroeconomic objectives. The success of government in achieving these targets requires sound statistical measures of the state of the economy and how it is performing.

Aggregate demand and aggregate supply: the determinants of output, employment and prices

This requires you to understand the components that make up aggregate demand and aggregate supply and the factors which influence their size and performance. In the same way that supply and demand analysis could be used to explain one market, their aggregated versions can be used to illustrate success and failure in achieving macroeconomic objectives.

The application of macroeconomic policy instruments

In order to achieve its macroeconomic objectives, the government has a variety of instruments at its disposal. To manipulate the demand side of the economy it can use monetary, fiscal and exchange rate policies, while an assortment of economic policies can be aggregated to boost the supply side of the economy. The process of economic management can produce conflicts. For example, the objective of slowing inflation may improve the balance of payments but worsen the level of employment and thereby slow economic growth.

Structure and essential determinants of international transactions

Although much of the preceding course content concentrates on the national economy, there is a long history of international trade between the UK and the rest of the world. This part of the course looks at why trade takes place and studies the costs and benefits of free and protected trade in international markets.

Government macroeconomic policy objectives and indicators of national economic performance

The indicators of national economic performance over the last 100 years have — even if we exclude exceptional periods like 1914–18 and 1939–45 — shown significant yearly variations such as:

- average level of prices falling by 10% in 1920 and rising by 30% in 1976
- the percentage of the workforce unemployed fluctuating from a high of 22% in 1932 to a low of 0.9% in 1955
- the balance of payments current account ranging between a deficit of £23 billion in 1989 to a £6 billion surplus in 1997
- economic growth rates ranging from –1.6% in 1975 to +5.2% in 1988

A 30% rate of inflation — coupled with high negative real rates of interest — creates significant redistributions of income and wealth and particularly hurts those people who live off their savings or who receive fixed incomes.

When 22% of the workforce is unemployed this creates poverty, reduces living standards, provokes social and industrial unrest and increases crime rates. It is not only the person who loses a job that is affected. Anyone who relies in whole or in part on his or her income is also affected.

Large fluctuations in the current account of the balance of payments can have significant distorting effects on the external rate of exchange and the prices of imports and exports.

Growth rates of 5% create expectations that standards of living are growing fast and when these do not materialise — as the growth rate becomes negative — this can have distorting effects on wage claims and expenditure plans.

The variations described above are dependent upon the reliability of the statistical techniques used to measure them.

Inflation rates are calculated from changes in the retail price index (RPI, which is known as the headline rate of inflation and RPIX, which excludes mortgage interest rates and is known as the underlying rate of inflation). Because of the immense task involved, the RPI cannot take account of all the price changes that take place in an economy over a given period of time. Instead, a shopping basket of representative products — chosen to reflect the average family — is measured. If you are not average, then these changes may not reflect the way that the value of the money you spend has changed.

Measures of unemployment may be significantly different from the number of people who are available to contribute to the productive process, but currently are not doing so. Over the years, governments have been astute at finding ways of removing people from the unemployment register. While this reduces the number counted as unemployed in official statistics, it does not necessarily mean that there are fewer people looking for work.

Errors and omissions in the balance of payments statistics require balancing items to produce an accounting equality. In addition, the demand for statistics to be produced as quickly as possible sometimes means that revised figures provided at a later date can show significant changes.

The growth rate of the economy is most commonly accounted for using gross domestic product (GDP). This can be measured in any of three ways:
- income
- output
- expenditure

Whichever measure is used, each one creates problems and although, in theory, they should produce the same total over the same period of time, this never happens in practice. Once again, estimates have to be used to cover statistical errors and omissions.

Finally, it is necessary to recognise the possibility of conflicting outcomes from the pursuit of a specific objective. For example, an attempt to boost economic growth may result in a rise in the rate of inflation and a worsening of the balance on current account.

Essential terms

You will need to be able to define the following essential terms:
- aggregate demand
- aggregate supply
- balance of payments
- circular flow of income
- demand management
- economic growth
- exchange rates
- fiscal policy
- gross domestic product
- inflation
- macroeconomics
- monetary policy
- nominal
- real
- supply-side economics
- unemployment

Understanding

You will need to understand the following:
- What is meant by the macroeconomic policy objectives of government and how these differ from other policies that are targeted at a particular sector of the economy.
- The reason why government establishes such objectives and the policy options available to achieve these goals.
- The difference between monetary policy (which targets the money supply and interest rates); fiscal policy (which uses the government's budget); exchange rate

policy (which changes the external value of the currency); and supply-side policies (which aim to boost output and productivity).

- The difference between nominal and real in measuring and valuing an economy. There must also be a recognition that the nominal and the real can move in opposite directions, as illustrated by a nominal rise in GDP which is less than the rate of inflation leading to a fall in real GDP.

Explanation

You will need to be able to explain the following:

- The four main government objectives of persistently low inflation, low levels of unemployment, long-term balance of payments equilibrium and sustainable economic growth.
- Different rates of inflation, the difference between accelerating and stable inflation, and between anticipated and unanticipated inflation.
- The various measures of employment and unemployment.
- The structure of the balance of payments, including the various components of the current account, the financial account (formerly known as the capital account) and the new capital account which includes only transactions in fixed assets. You will also need to explain the effect that changes in the balance of payments have on the exchange rate and vice versa.
- How economic growth is measured, the costs and benefits of economic growth and the advantages of sustainable growth.
- The three ways of measuring economic performance, i.e. income, output and expenditure, and the problems of getting the right information and making the correct interpretation.
- The use of index numbers to represent changes in economic performance and the method of calculating the retail price index.

Analysis

You will need to be able to analyse the following:

- The trends and breaks in trend for all the key economic indicators, i.e. inflation, unemployment, balance of payments, economic growth and GDP.
- Comparisons of economic performance between countries using the relevant data sets.
- The effect on the economy of changes to fiscal, monetary, exchange rate and supply-side policies. You will also need to show awareness of how changes in one policy may affect another, e.g. changes in fiscal policy will affect monetary policy.

Evaluation

You will need to be able to evaluate the following:

- The consequences for the economy of high rates of unemployment, high and accelerating inflation, balance of payments disequilibrium and slow or negative economic growth.

- The potential for conflict as government tries to pursue multiple policy targets, and the trade-offs that have to be made, e.g. a boost to economic growth damages the balance of payments.
- The macroeconomic policy objectives of government in terms of their expected outcome and their actual outcome, e.g. is there a conflict between quality of life and faster economic growth?

Check points

Be aware of the following points:
- Remember that there is considerable disagreement among those economists who insist that economic management is best pursued through demand-side policies and those who support the use of supply-side policies.
- If the government pursued an expansionary fiscal policy by budgeting for a deficit, this is likely to change monetary conditions as interest rates may have to be raised to finance the debt or the government's cash requirement may increase.
- The continued existence of macroeconomic problems suggests that governments do not have all the answers and may, through their actions, make problems worse rather than better.

Aggregate demand and aggregate supply: the determinants of output, employment and prices

In Unit 1 'The Market System' you will have studied the way in which markets are analysed using supply and demand curves to produce equilibrium prices and output conditions. In this part of the course you are looking at the economy as if it was one big market place. All the individual market demand curves are added together to produce an aggregate demand curve and all the market supply curves are used to produce an aggregate supply curve.

The aggregate demand curve slopes down from left to right meaning that if the average level of prices falls, then demand increases and vice versa. The components of aggregate demand (AD) in an economy are usually divided into:
- consumer expenditure (C)
- investment expenditure (I)
- government expenditure (G)
- export expenditure minus import expenditure (X – M)

This is symbolised as AD = C + I + G + X – M

The aggregate demand curve can shift to the left or right, if more or fewer products are demanded at the same average level of prices. This may occur as a result of a change in any of the determinants of consumption, investment, government spending or imports and exports.

The aggregate supply curve slopes upwards from left to right on the assumption that firms expand their output as prices rise and potential profits increase. Aggregate supply is dependent upon changes in the conditions for supplying products. For example, an improvement in technology may shift the curve to the right, while an increase in factor costs may shift it to the left. The slope of the aggregate supply curve varies dependent upon the underlying assumptions used in its construction. The normal aggregate supply curve (AS) is illustrated in diagram (a). At the extreme are theories that support either a curve which is perfectly inelastic (AS_1) at the given level of employed resources as in diagram (b), or a curve which is assumed to be perfectly elastic if the economy has unemployed resources to the point when all resources are fully employed where it becomes perfectly inelastic (AS_2). This is illustrated in diagram (c).

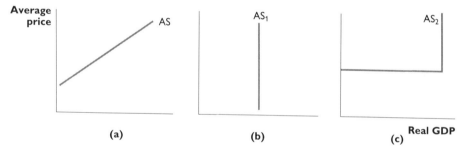

(a)   (b)   (c)

Macroeconomic equilibrium is illustrated by the intersection of the aggregate demand (AD) and aggregate supply curve (AS) as illustrated in the diagram below.

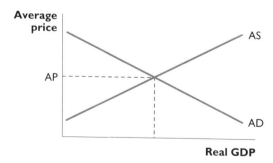

As with the market analysis developed in Unit 1 'The Market System', a shift in one curve causes a movement along the other. In this component of Unit 3, it is necessary to understand the circular flow of income. This is determined by the propensity to consume plus the injections of income into the flow that increase its value and the leakages (withdrawals) from the flow that have a reducing effect.

The main injections (J) and withdrawals (W) that affect the circular flow of income are paired into:

Injections	Withdrawals
Investment (I)	Savings (S)
Government expenditure (G)	Taxation (T)
Exports (X)	Imports (M)

Any change in the value of injections into or withdrawals from the circular flow of income have an effect which is greater than the original change. This is because income flows from one economic unit to another, and the difference between the final change in GDP and the original change in withdrawals or injections is measured by the multiplier.

Essential terms

You will need to be able to define the following essential terms:

- aggregate demand curve
- aggregate supply curve
- consumer expenditure
- exports
- general equilibrium
- government expenditure
- imports

- injections
- investment
- multiplier
- savings
- taxation
- withdrawal (leakage)

Understanding

You will need to understand the following:

- How the market mechanism allocates resources.
- The many markets in the economy that exist with or without government intervention and how policies can be pursued that affect the whole economy rather than any particular market within the economy.
- The difference between microeconomics and macroeconomics.

Explanation

You will need to be able to explain the following:

- Why the aggregate demand curve slopes downward from left to right, the normal aggregate supply curve and the extreme cases.
- The AS/AD model and what is meant by general equilibrium in terms of output and the average level of prices.
- The circular flow of income and the multiplier effect of injections into and withdrawals from the flow.

Analysis

You will need to be able to analyse the following:

- The shifts and movements in the aggregate demand and aggregate supply curves.

- How the general equilibrium position is affected by changes in the conditions of aggregate demand and aggregate supply.

Evaluation

You will need to be able to evaluate the usefulness of AD and AS models in understanding the main macroeconomic models in an economy.

Check points

Be aware of the following points:
- Remember that you can apply the logic learnt under supply, demand and markets to aggregate supply, aggregate demand and general equilibrium in a market economy.
- A shift in an aggregate demand or aggregate supply curve occurs when more or less is demanded or supplied at the same average level of prices, while a movement occurs when the average level of prices changes.

The application of macroeconomic policy instruments

In macroeconomic management there is a broad division between those policies that target the demand side of the economy and those that target the supply side. Fiscal and monetary policy aim to boost or suppress aggregate monetary demand. Supply-side policies focus on specific problems and solutions, including making labour markets more efficient through improved training and education, the creation of incentives to work harder and the reform of trade union law. Privatisation and deregulation have been used to encourage more competition.

Fiscal policy uses the balance between government expenditure and taxation to manipulate aggregate demand. More spending and/or less taxation produces an expansionary fiscal policy while a contractionary policy involves more taxation and/or less spending.

Monetary policy is concerned with adjustments to the supply of money in the economy and changes in the rate of interest. These can occur together or can be pursued independently, but even then it is not possible to separate the effects that interest rates have on money supply and vice versa.

Exchange rates are determined by supply and demand, and governments may intervene in the buying and selling of currency to pursue an exchange rate policy as part of their macroeconomic management.

The policies described above can be used separately or in concert to shift the aggregate demand and/or aggregate supply curves to a new position dependent upon which policy target has priority.

- To lower unemployment, expansionary fiscal and/or monetary policies shift the AD curve to the right. Over the longer term, supply-side policies could be used to shift the AS curve to the right.
- To lower inflation, contractionary fiscal and monetary policies could be used to remove the excessive monetary demand. Over the longer term, supply-side policies could be used to boost output, shift the AS curve to the right and absorb the excessive monetary demand.
- To remove a balance of payments current account deficit, contractionary fiscal and monetary policies could be used or exchange rates lowered. Over the longer term, supply-side policies could be used to promote exports and reduce imports.
- To promote economic growth, supply-side policies designed to boost productivity and improve technology could be pursued.

Essential terms

You will need to be able to define the following essential terms:

- balance of payments current account deficit
- deregulation
- interest rates
- money supply
- privatisation

Understanding

You will need to understand the following:

- What is meant by fiscal policy, monetary policy, exchange rate policy and supply-side economics.
- The difference between demand management and supply-side management of the economy.

Explanation

You will need to be able to explain:

- How fiscal policy can be used to change aggregate demand.
- The relationship between interest rates, money supply and aggregate monetary demand.
- The determination of an exchange rate using supply and demand curves for currency.
- The determination of interest rates using supply and demand curves for money.

Analysis

You will need to be able to analyse the way in which demand-side and supply-side policies can be used to shift aggregate demand and aggregate supply curves and their effect on the average level of prices and real GDP.

Evaluation

You will need to be able to evaluate the likely success of the policies chosen to achieve the macroeconomic objectives, and the conflicts that need to be reconciled.

Check points

Be aware of the following:

- Do not confuse fiscal and monetary policy. Remember, fiscal policy is concerned with taxation and expenditure, and monetary policy with the money supply and interest rates.
- Do not confuse changes in the balance between total taxation and expenditure (which are part of macroeconomic demand management) with adjustments to individual taxes and particular areas of expenditure that are part of supply-side policy. For example, a reduction in higher marginal rates of tax may be an attempt to motivate the workforce while increased expenditure on education and training is likely to be concerned with improving labour productivity. Neither need change the balance between taxation and expenditure and would therefore be supply-side policies.

Structure and essential determinants of international transactions

A closed economy is one that does not trade with other countries. The UK is an open economy exporting between one fifth and one quarter of its gross domestic product and importing a similar amount. Since the UK joined the European Economic Community (EEC) in 1973, the pattern of trade has shifted from its Commonwealth partner countries to the other members of what is now termed the European Union (EU). Over the same period, there has been a decline in the proportion of goods relative to services that are exported from the UK.

The theories of absolute advantage and comparative advantage explain not only the benefits of internal trade, but also those of international trade. Adam Smith (1723–90) explained the trade gains that occur when one country has absolute advantage in the production of some products and trades with other countries which have absolute advantage in the production of other products. David Ricardo (1772–1823) went one stage further and showed that there can still be gains from trade even if a country has an absolute disadvantage in the production of all products, so long as it has lower opportunity costs of production and therefore comparative advantage in the production of some products.

The main difference between internal trade and international trade is that internal trade is usually conducted in one currency and is relatively free from trade restrictions, whereas international trade is made more difficult by the need to trade currencies as well as products, and the degree to which countries protect themselves using options such as:

- tariffs
- quotas
- subsidies to domestic industry
- legislation
- quality control
- differential tax rates

The case for protection includes a variety of more or less sound economic arguments including:

- the protection of infant industries
- the protection of senile industries to allow them time to regenerate
- the countering of unfair trading practices such as dumping
- protection against illegal imports
- the protection of employment in industries sensitive to foreign competition
- a source of revenue for government

The case against protection includes:

- the advantages of free trade
- the problem that infant industries may never grow up and be able to compete
- the fact that protecting inefficient industry while it regenerates can lead to a permanent rather than temporary misallocation of resources
- the retaliations other countries may impose
- the rise in the cost of living and the restriction of consumer choice

Since the Second World War, there has been a concerted effort to lower trade barriers throughout the world. When countries joined the EU, they accepted free trade within its boundaries plus a common external tariff determined by the member country which originally had the lowest tariff with the rest of the world. In addition, the General Agreement on Tariffs and Trade (GATT), which was established in 1948, aimed to reduce protectionist measures between all countries in the world. This work was taken over by the World Trade Organisation (WTO) in 1995.

Essential terms

You will need to be able to define the following essential terms:

- absolute advantage
- comparative advantage
- dumping
- European Union
- free trade
- gains from trade
- infant industry
- international trade
- opportunity cost
- protection
- quota
- tariff
- World Trade Organisation

Understanding

You will need to understand the following:

- The pattern of trade between the UK and the EU, and the UK and the rest of the world, including some historical perspective on the broad changes that have taken place over time.
- The importance of imports and exports to the health of the UK economy, including knowledge of the main types of products traded internationally.

Explanation

You will need to be able to explain:

- The gains that economies can make through engaging in international trade. Brief reference may be made to absolute and comparative advantage, but it will not be necessary to produce numerical examples.
- The advantages of free trade as opposed to the resource misallocation that takes place behind trade barriers.
- The various tariff and non-tariff methods of protecting the domestic economy from potential problems caused by free international trade.

Analysis

You will need to be able to use a supply and demand analysis to illustrate the various equilibriums that may exist in an economy as illustrated in the diagram below.

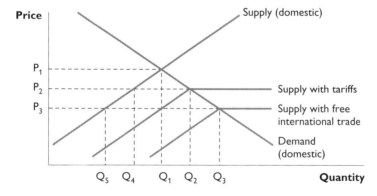

P_1Q_1 = no international trade
P_2Q_2 = trade behind a tariff barrier
P_3Q_3 = free trade

In the example, also note that domestic supply is Q_1 with no international trade and falls back to Q_4 with tariffs and Q_5 with free trade.

In addition to the above, you will need to be able to analyse the impact that membership of the European Union has had on the pattern of UK trade.

Evaluation

You will need to be able to evaluate the arguments for and against trading products freely throughout the world as opposed to the erection of trade barriers that are used to protect economies.

Check points

Be aware of the following:

- The need to be clear about when things happened, e.g. the date that the UK joined the EEC (1973) and when the EEC became the EU (1993).
- The need to familiarise yourself with the representation of data in the form of graphs and tables as this is how they may be presented in the examination.

Questions
&
Answers

In this section of the guide there are six questions, each followed by two sample answers interspersed with examiner's comments.

Questions

There are six case study examination papers which are constructed to reflect the AS format. To increase the range of topics covered the last question on each paper offers an either/or option. Whichever option is chosen, the question must be answered in continuous prose and it includes marks for quality of written communication. As a whole, this paper accounts for 40% of the AS total mark and 20% of the A-level total mark. The time allocated to reading the case study and answering the questions is 1 hour. The questions in each examination paper range across the entire AS specification for Module 2883. They test a hierarchy of skills which starts with definitions and basic understanding of the 'National and International Economy' and its specialised language, and progresses to include your ability to explain this knowledge. Beyond this, the higher-level skills of application, analysis and evaluation are tested.

Mark schemes

These are similar to those an examiner would use to complete the initial marking of a script. Each scheme highlights the points that will score marks. However, they are for guidance and do not necessarily illustrate the only correct interpretation. Some answers may be different and equally valid and would therefore be awarded equal marks. The mark schemes are designed to help you to focus your attention on what the examiner is looking for in the award of marks. Do not be tempted to read these mark schemes before you attempt to answer the questions. Use these examination papers as if they were the real thing.

Sample answers and examiner comments

After each question and mark scheme there are two scripts that reflect the answers required for the award of a grade A and a grade C. The grade A answers are not perfect, but are sufficient to achieve 80% or more, while the grade C answers have some errors and omissions that cause them to score between 60 and 69%. Throughout the sample answers, examiner comments are preceded by the icon ℮. These comments reflect the strengths and weaknesses of answers as well as pointing out common errors which have been made by many students in the past, but should not be made by you in the future.

Time allowed: 1 hour

Read the case study below. Answer parts (a) to (c). Choose either (d) (i) or (d) (ii) and write your answer in continuous prose. There are quality of written communication marks in (d) only.

Total marks allocated: 45.

International economic comparisons

Table 1 A comparison of the UK and Ethiopia

1998	GDP per capita ($)	GDP per capita (PPP$)	Human development index	External debt (% of GDP)
Ethiopia	100	500	0.298	131
UK	21,400	20,640	0.918	0

In order to compare the UK and Ethiopia, it is necessary to convert domestic currencies into a common currency. As the Ethiopian currency is not traded on the foreign exchange market, the official government rate is used. To make a clearer comparison of living standards, the United Nations International Comparison Project has produced an alternative set of exchange rates. These are measured as purchasing power parity figures (PPP$) and are illustrated in Table 1. They represent an attempt to equalise the spending power of each domestic currency.

Table 2 shows a comparison over 3 years of three key variables between the UK and US.

Table 2 A comparison of the UK and US (%)

	1997	1998	1999
UK			
Growth	3.5	2.1	3.0
Inflation	2.9	2.3	2.1
Interest rates	7.0	7.4	5.4
US			
Growth	3.9	4.3	4.2
Inflation	2.4	1.6	2.2
Interest rates	5.7	5.5	5.1

(a) The following economic terms are used in the description. Explain what is meant by:
  (i) GDP per capita   (2 marks)
  (ii) foreign exchange market   (2 marks)
  (iii) interest rate   (2 marks)

(b) (i) Explain why the **GDP** per capita in Ethiopia is considerably different when measured in **US** dollars compared with **GDP** per capita (**PPP$**), and why the **UK GDP** per capita totals are very similar. (5 marks)

(ii) The human development index (**HDI**) is calculated using three criteria, only one of which relates to the spending power of a person's income. Choose any two additional criteria that you think should be included in a development index and explain your choice. (6 marks)

(iii) Based on **GDP** per capita ($), what is the value of external debt per person in Ethiopia and the **UK**? (2 marks)

(iv) In respect of interest rates, explain one disadvantage of having a large external debt. (2 marks)

(c) (i) Given only the statistics in Table 2, explain why the growth rate in the **US** is faster than in the **UK**. (6 marks)

(ii) Explain how the rate of inflation is calculated in the **UK**. (6 marks)

(d) **Either:**

(i) Evaluate the problems of using **GDP** statistics to measure differences in living standards over time in the same country, and at one point in time between countries. (12 marks)

or:

(ii) Discuss the ways in which government can manage an economy to encourage economic growth. (12 marks)

■ ■ ■

Mark scheme

(a) (i) A measure of the domestic output of an economy over a given period of time divided by the population (2 marks).

(ii) A market where foreign currencies are traded and the price is determined by the supply of and the demand for each individual currency (2 marks).

(iii) An interest rate is the cost of borrowing money, or the price of capital, or the reward for parting with liquidity (2 marks).

(b) (i) Look for an explanation of how a currency traded freely on the foreign exchange market will more closely reflect its purchasing power than a currency which is fixed by a government and not traded internationally (5 marks).

(ii) The two HDI criteria are (a) literacy and school enrolment and (b) life expectancy, but allow any two justified criteria (2 × 3 marks).

(iii) Ethiopia = $131 (1 mark), UK = $0 (1 mark).

(iv) May include the need to earn foreign currency to service the debt or the possible variations that take place in interest rates over time (2 marks).

(c) (i) It is necessary to identify the growth rates for the UK and US, pointing out the faster rate of growth in the US (2 marks). Identify the lower rates of inflation and explain the possible effect on growth (2 marks). Identify the lower rates of interest and explain the possible effect on growth (2 marks).

(ii) An explanation of the retail price index is sufficient and, in addition to the final calculation, should point out that:
- a representative basket of products is chosen
- each item is given the index number 100 in a base year
- each item is weighted dependent on the pattern of consumer expenditure
- percentage changes are added or taken away from the index number

(6 marks)

(d) Either:

(i) Expect an answer which evaluates the problems over time to include some of the following:
- population changes
- variations in statistical calculation
- changes in money value
- balance of payments disequilibriums
- distribution of income and wealth
- changes in working conditions
- exceptional years
- externalities

and the problems between countries to include differences in some of the following:
- currencies
- methods of collection
- distribution of income and wealth
- non-marketed resources
- leisure times
- defence budgets
- externalities

(9 marks + 3 marks for quality of written communication)

or:

(ii) Expect an explanation of what is meant by economic growth and how the government can use its macroeconomic policies — including fiscal, monetary, exchange rate and supply side — to create an economic environment that will foster growth or be actively involved in trying to stimulate growth (9 marks + 3 marks for quality of written communication).

■ ■ ■

Response to question 1: grade A answer

(a) (i) GDP stands for gross domestic product, and it is a measure of the total output of any economy usually measured over one year. This total is then divided by the number of people in the country to get a per capita figure.

2/2 marks

(ii) The foreign exchange market is made up of many firms which buy and sell the currencies of the more developed countries. The price of a currency is established by the supply of currency (which is determined by the demand for imports) and the demand for currency (which is determined by the demand for exports).

2/2 marks

e An excellent answer, although perhaps it goes into more detail than is required to achieve full marks.

(ii) The rate of interest is what is charged to a borrower for a loan and what is paid to a saver to compensate for parting with liquidity. It is usually referred to as a rate per annum.

2/2 marks

(b) (i) If the Ethiopian currency is not traded on foreign exchange markets, then people who travel to Ethiopia will probably have to buy domestic currency at a rate fixed by the government. It is likely, in the case of Ethiopia, that this rate is significantly different from a rate that would reflect the buying power of the currency. However, in the UK, sterling is traded on the foreign exchange market and it is likely that the market rate will reflect the buying power of the currency; otherwise there would be a significant distortion in the price of UK products in foreign markets and vice versa.

5/5 marks

(ii) The life expectancy and proportion of children surviving until the age of five can indicate a more or a less advanced country.

2/6 marks

e The candidate identifies two relevant criteria but does not offer an explanation of either.

(iii) Ethiopia — external debt is 131% of 100 = 131
UK — external debt is 0% of 21,400 = 0

2/2 marks

(iv) A large external debt means that a country will have to sell products abroad to earn the foreign currency to finance this debt.

2/2 marks

(c) (i) The growth rate in the US may be faster because the interest rate is lower and therefore there will be more investment. Also, inflation is lower and this creates a more stable economic environment.

4/6 marks

e The candidate identifies that interest rates are lower and that this could lead to more investment (2 marks) and also that inflation is lower and this will cause more stability (2 marks). These points would need to be expanded for a higher mark.

(ii) In the UK inflation is usually measured by using the retail price index. This index selects 600 items and asks approximately 7,000 households to keep a record of the price paid for these items and how much is spent on them. Each item is given a base number and weights are allocated to the item dependent on the proportion spent by consumers. Percentage changes in price are added to or taken away from the index number and a new retail price average index is calculated by multiplying each index number by its weight, then adding up the new index number for each item and dividing by the number of weights.

6/6 marks

(d) (i) The statistics for gross domestic product have not always been available and therefore they can only be used to compare changes over time in the same country relatively recently. Also, the size of the population has changed so GDP figures only become meaningful if they are per capita figures.

Over time the quality and range of products purchased has changed and this will change living standards, but is not reflected in raw figures.

Inflation means that nominal figures are meaningless and a GDP deflator will have to be used so that the statistics reflect real changes in GDP.

Over the years, there will have been changes in working conditions and working practices which will have improved life at work as well as increased the number of leisure hours and reduced working hours. These changes will not have been registered in higher incomes, but they will have increased standards of living.

Between countries there must be an adjustment to a common currency in order to make comparisons. Also, there is a difficulty to overcome where exchange rates do not reflect purchasing power in each country.

From one country to another the methods of collecting statistics vary, with different countries relying on sampling to a greater or lesser extent. Also, non-marketed products will vary from one country to another. In Singapore, it is not necessary to spend money on heating whereas it commands a significant amount of expenditure in Iceland.

Defence budgets vary from one country to another and the larger the proportion of GDP spent on defence, the lower the living standards.

6/9 + 3/3 marks

e The answer is well written and achieves maximum quality of written communication marks. It could have done with a little fleshing out with an explanation of standard of living and a concluding statement.

Scored 36/45 80% = Grade A

■ ■ ■

Response to question 1: grade C answer

(a) (i) GDP per capita is gross domestic product per person.

1/2 marks

e The candidate says what the term is, but offers no explanation.

(ii) The foreign exchange market is where different currencies are bought and sold.
1/2 marks

e The candidate offers limited explanation.

(iii) The interest rate is the price that has to be paid for taking out a loan.
1/2 marks

e The candidate gives limited coverage.

(b) (i) In Ethiopia, the gross domestic product per capita measured in terms of dollars is 4.6% of the GDP figure for the UK. However, when it is measured in terms of the purchasing power of each domestic currency, it is recorded as 24.4% of the UK figure. This means that the people in Ethiopia are significantly better off using the PPP$ calculation than is implied by the raw exchange rate. This may be because the government is intervening in the market for foreign currency.
4/5 marks

e This reasonable attempt at an answer loses a mark through not referring to the use of an official government rate in Ethiopia.

(ii) Life expectancy varies considerably from the more developed to the less developed countries where the average age of death can be in the 30s. As people's real income rises, so they buy cars and therefore a calculation of population size divided by the number of cars in a country would indicate how far they had developed.
6/6 marks

(iii) $131 in Ethiopia and zero in the UK.
2/2 marks

(iv) Over time, interest rates can rise and fall considerably so that a country with a large external debt will have to pay large variable payments to service the debt.
2/2 marks

(c) (i) The growth rate in the UK was lower than the US because the rate of inflation was higher and the interest rate in two out of the three years was higher. A higher interest rate is likely to mean less consumer demand in the UK, and a higher rate of inflation may have been caused by a rise in the costs of production which has made the UK economy less competitive.
3/6 marks

e The answer does not consider the benefits of lower rates for inflation and interest in the US.

(ii) It is usual to measure the rate of inflation using the retail price index (RPI). The RPI is calculated using a basket of products which are consumed by the average family. Percentage changes in prices and weights are added to each product and then an average for all the products in the basket is calculated.
3/6 marks

e The description is too brief and there is some uncertainty over the way in which weights are used in the index.

(d) (ii) There are four main ways that government can manage an economy. These are:
- fiscal policy
- monetary policy
- exchange rate policy
- supply-side policy

Using fiscal policy — which changes the balance of expenditure and taxation — the government can budget for a deficit and boost aggregate demand to stimulate economic activity.

Monetary policy is using interest rates and changes in the money supply to stimulate demand and encourage investment. An expansion in the money supply and lower interest rates will make investment in capital more attractive.

Exchange rate policy can have an uncertain effect on economic growth, as lowering exchange rates may boost export sales but at the same time raise the cost of imports.

On the supply side of the economy the government can do things to boost economic growth such as:
- lower taxes to motivate the workforce
- improve education and training
- improve the infrastructure

5/9 + 2/3 marks

e The answer is brief and tends to explain rather than discuss points. A discussion involves at least two sides to the argument. Also, although it is reasonably well written, a quality of written communication mark is lost because the continuous prose, which the examiner expects, is punctuated by lists.

Scored 30/45 66.7% = Grade C

Time allowed: 1 hour

Read the case study below. Answer parts (a) to (c). Choose either (d) (i) or (d) (ii) and write your answer in continuous prose. There are quality of written communication marks in (d) only.

Total marks allocated: 45.

International trade

Table 1 UK balance of payments (£m)

	Balance of trade	Invisible balance	Other balances	Current balance
1996	−13,086	8,897	3,589	−600
1997	−11,910	12,414	6,119	6,623
1998	−20,537	12,124	7,758	−655
1999	−26,611	11,114	2,736	−12,761

Table 2 Comparisons between the UK and Japan

	Exchange rate (yen/£)	Consumer price index (1995 = 100)		GDP growth rate (%)	
		UK	Japan	UK	Japan
1996	170	102.4	100.1	2.5	3.9
1997	198	105.7	101.8	3.5	0.9
1998	217	109.3	102.5	2.1	−2.5
1999	184	110.0	102.2	3.0	0.3

The UK balance of payments showed a marked improvement on the current balance between 1996 and 1997 and then deteriorated in 1998–99. Throughout the period, the UK had run a tight fiscal policy and a more expansionary monetary policy. In comparison, Japan had become worried about economic recession and lowered its interest rates to 0.2%.

(a) Explain what is meant by the following economic terms:
    (i) balance of trade   (2 marks)
    (ii) current balance   (2 marks)
    (iii) economic recession   (2 marks)
    (iv) investment   (2 marks)

(b) (i) The balance of payments will always produce a zero balance. Explain this statement and identify what is missing from the statistics in Table 1.   (4 marks)
    (ii) 'A tight fiscal policy and a more expansionary monetary policy' is quoted above. Explain what is meant by this statement.   (4 marks)
    (iii) Describe what is meant by a current balance deficit and current balance surplus and say whether it would be possible for a country to be continuously in deficit on its current account.   (6 marks)

(c) (i) Using only evidence from Tables 1 and 2, suggest reasons for the changes that have taken place in the value of the yen to the pound between 1996 and 1999. (6 marks)

(ii) What evidence in Table 2 explains why Japan is worried about recession and what effect is lowering interest rates to 0.2% likely to have on the Japanese economy? (3 marks)

(iii) If the rate of interest in Japan was 0.2% in 1996–97, explain whether the real rate of interest was positive or negative. (2 marks)

(d) Either:

(i) Explain how the exchange rate of a country is determined and identify the factors that may cause the rate to change. (12 marks)

or:

(ii) Despite the advantages of free trade, almost all countries have protected themselves to a greater or lesser extent from totally free trade. Identify the main trade barriers and discuss whether such protection is a benefit to an economy. (12 marks)

Mark scheme

(a) (i) Must show clear understanding that a balance is the difference between two totals, in this case goods exported and imported (2 marks).

(ii) The two totals are goods and services exported and imported (2 marks).

(iii) A downturn in economic activity that may lead to a depression (2 marks). Alternatively, the student may refer to the more precise measure of two successive quarters of negative economic growth.

(iv) Needs to refer to the purchase of capital goods (2 marks).

(b) (i) For an explanation of the accounting identity (3 marks). For recognising that the financial account or capital account or balancing item is missing (1 mark). To get the mark it is OK to make reference to only one item.

(ii) For an explanation of tight fiscal policy (2 marks) and expansionary monetary policy (2 marks).

(iii) Current balance deficit (2 marks), current balance surplus (2 marks). An explanation of why it would be difficult for a country to run a persistent deficit in terms of limited foreign exchange reserves and a limited ability to borrow foreign currency (2 marks).

(c) (i) It is necessary to explain that the rise in the pound and fall in the yen between 1996 and 1998 may have been the result of improving current balance, and faster growth rate in the UK, while the reverse in 1999 may have been the result of a significant worsening in the current balance and higher inflation (6 marks). To achieve full marks, it is necessary to recognise the break in trend in 1999.

(ii) Look for any two of the following: deteriorating and negative growth rate; the fall in the consumer price index; or the rise in the external value of the currency (2 marks). The lowering of interest rates may be aimed at boosting investment and increasing consumer demand (1 mark).

(iii) The real rate of interest is negative (1 mark) because the rate of inflation is higher than the rate of interest (1 mark).

(d) Either:

  (i) Allocate approximately half marks to an explanation (supported by a diagram) of how an exchange rate is determined in a free market through the interaction of supply and demand. The answer may include a reference to fixed and floating rates. The other half of the marks is allocated to identifying the factors which shift either the supply curve or the demand curve for currency and produce a new equilibrium rate (9 + 3 marks for quality of written communication).

or:

  (ii) Expect a brief mention of the gains from trade that derive from the specialisation of function (2 marks). For identifying the main trade barriers (3 marks) and for discussing the economic advantages and disadvantages (4 marks, plus 3 marks for quality of written communication)..

■ ■ ■

Response to question 2: grade A answer

(a) (i) The balance of trade is the difference between the total value of exported goods and the total value of imported goods over a given period of time. It does not include trade in services.
2/2 marks

  (ii) The current balance is the difference between the total value of exported goods and services and the total value of imported goods and services over a given period of time.
2/2 marks

  (iii) An economic recession is usually described as a slowdown or downturn in economic activity. This may be characterised by rising unemployment, falling incomes and an increase in bankruptcies.
2/2 marks

  (iv) Investment is when a person sets aside some income to buy stocks and shares in order to receive dividends and make a capital gain.
0/2 marks

  _e_ The candidate makes a common mistake here. Remember that in economics investment refers to the buying of capital goods like machinery.

(b) (i) When people buy imports, they supply their currency to buy foreign currency. When foreigners want to buy UK exports, they supply their currency to buy the exporter's currency. In the UK, if there is not sufficient foreign currency to be bought, then the official reserves have to be run down or foreign currency has to be borrowed. The result of this is that all the unofficial trades in the balance of payments will have to be matched by an official adjustment to currencies that will produce an overall zero balance. In the statistics in Table 1, the capital account and financial account are missing.
4/4 marks

(ii) Fiscal policy is using the government's budget to manage the overall level of economic activity. A tight fiscal policy occurs when the government reduces expenditure and/or increases taxation in order to reduce aggregate demand. An expansionary monetary policy takes place when the Bank of England reduces interest rates in an attempt to boost aggregate monetary demand.
3/4 marks

In answering this question the candidate is expected to make reference to increasing the money supply as well as reducing interest rates under an expansionary monetary policy.

(iii) A current balance deficit occurs on the balance of payments when the value of imported goods and services exceeds the value of exported goods and services over a given period of time. This situation is reversed for a current balance surplus when the value of exported goods and services is greater than the corresponding imports.

Many countries, including the UK and the US, have run current balance deficits for long periods of time, but technically it is not possible to persistently run a deficit because there are limited foreign exchange reserves in a country. Also, a persistent deficit is likely to lead to a fall in the exchange rate and this makes it more difficult to borrow foreign currencies as foreign countries lose confidence in the country's ability to maintain the value of its currency.
6/6 marks

(c) (i) The value of the pound against the yen rose between 1996 and 1998 from 170 yen to the pound to 217 yen to the pound. The reason for this may have been the improving current balance on the balance of payments, particularly between 1996 and 1997. Also, the growth rate was considerably higher in the UK between 1997 and 1998.

However, between 1998 and 1999 the value of sterling fell from 217 yen to 184 yen. This may be because inflation was much higher in the UK and deflation had actually taken place in Japan. Also, the UK's current account of the balance of payments had nose-dived into a deficit of nearly £13 billion.
6/6 marks

(ii) Japan is worried about the likelihood of an economic recession because the consumer price index indicates a deflation falling from 102.5 to 102.2 and the exchange rate has increased in value meaning that Japan will find it more difficult to sell abroad.
2/3 marks

The candidate has not attempted to explain the effect of lower interest rates on the Japanese economy.

(iii) Between 1996 and 1997 the consumer price index rose by $1.7/100.1 \times 100 = 1.6983\%$, while the rate of interest was only 0.2%. Therefore the real interest rate was a negative 1.5%.
2/2 marks

(d) (ii) There are many ways that a country can choose to protect itself against imports. The most commonly used trade barrier is to impose a tariff on all or selected imports. The tariff is like a tax and it can be a specific amount or an ad valorem tariff. The revenue collected goes to the Treasury.

A second fairly common method of protection is to impose a quota on a foreign country or a foreign product. This limits the quantity that can be imported over a specific period of time and can often benefit firms which have a share of the quota as the restricted supply allows them to raise prices and increase profit margins.

A variety of domestic policies can be used to protect domestic industry and disadvantage potential competition from abroad. A government may choose to subsidise domestic industry and this will allow it to undercut the price of imports. It is possible to use legislation to protect domestic industry. In Tokyo, only Japanese-made cars were allowed to use the public car parks which made people think twice about buying a foreign car. It is also possible to use differential tax rates to disadvantage imports. The small Japanese car is a few centimetres narrower than its European competitors which are then taxed at a higher rate because they are larger cars.

Finally, it is also possible to appeal to the patriotic nature of a country and discourage imports. French farmers have been particularly effective in discouraging farm products from the UK, while the UK has, in the past, used 'Buy British' campaigns to encourage consumers to buy British products.
4/9 + 3/3 marks

The answer is well written, but the candidate has not fully addressed the question. The main trade barriers have been identified, but there is little discussion of what benefits these have for the economy, e.g.:

- to protect infant industry
- to allow senile industry to regenerate
- to counter unfair trading practices
- to protect against illegal imports
- national security
- to preserve UK jobs

Scored 36/45 80% = Grade A

■ ■ ■

Response to question 2: grade C answer

(a) (i) The balance of trade is a measure of all the imports and exports of a country.
0/2 marks

The candidate does not identify what is meant by a balance or isolate goods only.

(ii) The current balance measures the state of the balance of payments including all capital transactions.
0/2 marks

This answer should not include capital transactions.

(iii) An economic recession means that output is falling, unemployment is rising and incomes are falling. It often comes before a depression and after a boom.
2/2 marks

(iv) Investment takes place when current consumption is foregone and resources are allocated to the production of factories and machines.
2/2 marks

(b) (i) The balance of payments will always produce a zero balance. This is because the value of everything leaving the country in the form of exports must be equal to the value of everything entering the country. Any shortfall of foreign currency will be made up from the government's foreign exchange reserves. There is something missing from Table 1 because the numbers in each year do not add up to zero.
2/4 marks

e The candidate does not know what is missing from Table 1. The first part of the answer is not particularly well explained, although it does show some understanding.

(ii) Taxation is a withdrawal from the circular flow of income while expenditure is an injection. Fiscal policy is using the budget to change the overall level of aggregate demand in the economy. If more money is withdrawn from the economy by taxation than is injected into the economy, then it would be described as a tight fiscal policy. An expansionary monetary policy is one that would allow the money supply to expand and interest rates to fall. This would expand aggregate monetary demand in the economy.
4/4 marks

(iii) A current balance deficit is when the balance of payments shows a deficit before any official financing, whereas a surplus does not require official financing. It would not be possible for a country to run a current balance deficit continually as it has neither sufficient reserves of foreign currency to fill the gap, nor unlimited capacity to borrow from other countries.
2/6 marks

e The candidate does not understand what is meant by a current balance surplus or deficit, but is awarded marks for commenting on whether a deficit can be continuously run.

(c) (i) The value of the yen fell between 1996 — when 170 yen were required to buy a pound — and 1998 — when 217 yen were needed. This may have occurred as a result of the relative strength of the pound and a strengthening current balance. Also, the UK economy was growing faster than the Japanese economy. Between 1998 and 1999 the situation reversed as the yen rose in value against the pound. This may have been because of a significant worsening in the UK current balance and a relatively high rate of inflation in the UK. Also, the Japanese economy was starting to grow again.
6/6 marks

question

(ii) The Japanese are worried about a recession because the growth rate of GDP has become negative (–2.5% in 1998). Lowering interest rates may encourage investment and help to increase the growth rate.

2/3 marks

 The candidate misses evidence from the consumer price index and the effect of a lower interest rate on consumer spending.

(iii) The real rate of interest is a positive number, i.e. 0.2%.

0/2 marks

 The candidate does not understand what is meant by 'real'.

(d) (i) The exchange rate of a country is determined by the supply of currency to the foreign exchange market and the demand from the same market. Supply of currency is determined by the demand for imports, while the demand for currency is determined by the demand for exports. In the diagram below, the price of a currency is measured by another currency, and the intersection of the supply and demand curve is the equilibrium exchange rate.

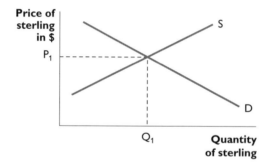

The factors that may cause the exchange rate to change are those that will shift either the supply curve or the demand curve for currency. The demand curve of currency to buy exports and the supply curve of currency to buy imports may shift as the result of:
- a change in taste for UK products abroad and foreign products at home
- different inflation rates between countries
- different rates of economic growth
- different interest rates between countries

6/9 + 2/3 marks

 The first part of the answer is well written and scores 6 marks. The second part of the answer includes a list which is not developed and this cannot be used as a substitute for an explanation in continuous prose. The points made are relevant and score 2 marks, while a quality of written communication mark is lost, giving 2/3 marks.

Scored 28/45 62.2% = Grade C

question Q3

Time allowed: 1 hour

Read the case study below. Answer parts (a) to (c). Choose either (d) (i) or (d) (ii) and write your answer in continuous prose. There are quality of written communication marks in (d) only.

Total marks allocated: 45.

Changing attitudes to macroeconomic management

Over the last 50 years, there has been considerable discussion over whether the economy can be fine tuned by manipulating aggregate demand to achieve full employment and stable prices. Fiscal policy has been the main tool of macroeconomic management with an accommodating monetary policy. Critics of this view of macroeconomic management have suggested that there are too many unknown and unpredictable reactions in the economy to the rather blunt tool of demand-side management. These economists have tended to suggest that on the demand side of the economy the best we can hope for is a steady expansion in aggregate demand roughly in line with the growth in output of the economy. If this is the situation, then how do we deal with problems such as slow, sluggish and even negative economic growth? Is there a solution to the problem identified in Figure 1 below?

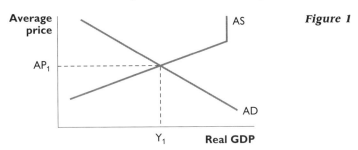

Figure 1

Here, the current equilibrium situation for the economy is at $Y_1 AP_1$. The economy has a relatively high level of unemployment and is not achieving its full productive potential which is to the right of Y_1. An alternative view put forward by other economists is that the government should adopt and promote supply-side policies that will shift the supply curve outward to achieve equilibrium at a higher level of economic activity.

(a) Briefly answer the following questions:

    (i) What is meant by an economy's productive potential? (2 marks)

    (ii) What is the difference between an aggregate supply curve and an aggregate demand curve? (2 marks)

    (iii) Distinguish between monetary and fiscal policy. (3 marks)

    (iv) What is meant by the statement 'fiscal policy has been the main tool of macroeconomic management with an accommodating monetary policy'? (3 marks)

question

(b) (i) Identify the four main components of aggregate demand. (4 marks)

(ii) Explain why the aggregate demand curve in Figure 1 is downward sloping from left to right. (4 marks)

(iii) Explain what is meant by a person's disposable income and their marginal propensity to consume. (2 marks)

(iv) With reference to the 'marginal propensity to consume', explain how it may cause a shift in the aggregate demand curve. (3 marks)

(c) (i) Explain, with the use of a diagram, an outward shift in an aggregate supply curve and offer two reasons that explain why the curve may have shifted to the right. (6 marks)

(ii) The equilibrium position for the economy, as illustrated in Figure 1 by Y_1, can be disturbed by injections into the circular flow and leakages from the circular flow. Identify the three main injections and the three main leakages from the circular flow, and state whether it is more likely that they will have an initial impact on the aggregate demand curve or the aggregate supply curve. (4 marks)

(d) Either:

(i) (a) How is unemployment measured? (4 marks)

(b) Discuss the arguments for using either demand management or supply-side policies to reduce the problem of unused productive potential. (8 marks)

or:

(ii) What is sustainable economic growth? Evaluate either the costs or the benefits of achieving a high rate of economic growth. (12 marks)

Mark scheme

(a) (i) Explain the full use of an economy's productive factors. The answer may include a production possibility boundary (2 marks).

(ii) An explanation of the upward-sloping supply curve (1 mark) and the downward-sloping demand curve (1 mark).

(iii) Monetary policy (1 mark), fiscal policy (1 mark) and a distinguishing comment (1 mark).

(iv) An explanation in terms of how the government has used the difference between taxation and expenditure to manage the economy and the possible effect it could have on monetary policy (3 marks).

(b) (i) Consumer expenditure (1 mark), government expenditure (1 mark), investment (1 mark), the balance between exports and imports (1 mark).

(ii) An explanation may include the increased foreign demand for exports at lower prices, the real income effect of falling prices, the wealth effect of falling prices, and the expectations of rises in the future (4 marks). At least two of the above explained well can gain maximum marks.

(iii) Explain disposable income (1 mark), and marginal propensity to consume (1 mark).

(iv) Explain a shift and say how an increase or decrease in the marginal propensity to consume can change consumer expenditure, which is the main component of aggregate demand (3 marks).

(c) (i) An explanation of any two of the following: (4 marks)
- increased investment and business
- increased technical efficiency, invention and innovation
- improved training and education
- increased incentive to work and work harder
- improvements in geographical and occupational mobility

Plus a labelled diagram to illustrate (2 marks).

(ii) Savings and investment (1 mark), taxation and government expenditure (1 mark), imports and exports (1 mark), likely to affect aggregate demand (1 mark).

(d) Either:

(i) (a) Common measures include those who register for unemployment benefits and the sample 'Labour Force Survey'. Other measures may be included (3 marks + 1 mark for quality of written communication).

(b) It will be necessary to explain how fiscal, monetary and exchange rate policies can be used to manipulate aggregate demand, including some assessment of their likely efficacy. Or the impact of supply-side policies, including the likelihood of their success (6 marks + 2 marks for quality of written communication).

or:

(ii) The candidate must identify sustainability as well as offer some evaluation of either the likely costs or benefits of a high rate of economic growth, which may or may not be considered sustainable (9 marks + 3 marks for quality of written communication).

■ ■ ■

Response to question 3: grade A answer

(a) (i) At any one point in time, an economy has a finite capacity to produce goods and services given its factors of production. This is called its productive potential and can be illustrated by a production possibility boundary. If a country has unemployed resources, then it is producing below its productive potential.

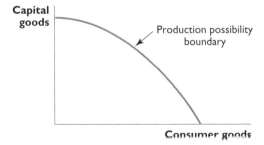

2/2 marks

(ii) An aggregate supply curve illustrates the functional relationship between the real GDP and the average level of prices. It is upward sloping, meaning that at higher average prices more output is produced. In contrast, the aggregate demand curve is downward sloping meaning that at lower average prices more will be demanded.
2/2 marks

question

(iii) Monetary policy is when the Bank of England uses interest rates and its controls over the money supply to manage the overall level of monetary demand. In contrast, the Treasury is concerned with overseeing fiscal policy, which is using the budget to change the overall balance between taxation and expenditure and therefore the overall level of aggregate demand.

3/3 marks

(iv) The statement means that the government has been mainly concerned with managing the demand-side of the economy using budget deficits to expand the economy and surpluses to dampen down demand. These policies tend to have a secondary effect on monetary policy, e.g. a budget deficit could cause interest rates to rise to finance the borrowing requirement.

3/3 marks

(b) (i) The main components of aggregate demand are consumer expenditure, government expenditure and investment expenditure.

3/4 marks

 The candidate missed out exports–imports.

(ii) The aggregate demand curve is downward sloping from left to right because — as the average level of prices falls — more foreigners are attracted to buy UK products. People in the UK would find an increase in their real income at lower prices, and also a substitution effect as UK consumers find domestic products cheaper to buy than the competing imported product.

4/4 marks

(iii) Disposable income is what is left over to spend after a person's total income is reduced by claims in the form of taxation, national insurance and pensions. The marginal propensity to consume (MPC) is how much of an additional pound received a consumer will spend. If it is 80p then MPC = 80p/100p = 0.8.

2/2 marks

(iv) If we assume that the marginal propensity to consume is 0.8 and something happens to reduce it to 0.7, then this will reduce consumer expenditure. As consumer expenditure is the main component of aggregate demand, so the aggregate demand curve shifts to the left. The reverse happens if the MPC increases.

3/3 marks

(c) (i)

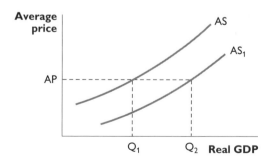

An outward shift in the aggregate supply curve means that more output is being supplied at each and every average price. This may be caused by increases in investment, or the invention of new products.
4/6 marks

e The diagram scores 2, but the two reasons are stated rather than explained. Therefore the candidate loses 2 marks.

(ii) Consumer expenditure, government expenditure, investment, savings, taxation and imports. Changes in any of these will affect the aggregate demand curve.
2/4 marks

e Consumer expenditure is not an injection and mention of exports is missed out.

(d) (i) (a) The level of unemployment in the economy is recorded by adding together all those people who register as unemployed and therefore claim benefits. This means that unemployment is probably understated, because people who do not claim these benefits are not included in the statistics. Also, surveys are carried out in selected proportions of the population from which estimates of unemployment can be made.
3/3 + 1/1 marks

(b)

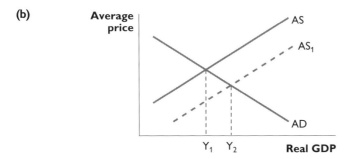

In the diagram above, Y_1 represents the current equilibrium position for an economy with unused productive potential. Y_2 represents the position where all resources are fully employed. To reach this point using supply-side policies, the AS curve will need to shift its position to AS_1.

Over recent years there seems to have been a move to using supply-side policies to motivate the worker and the firm into working harder. This may involve lowering marginal rates of taxation or corporation tax. It could be done through education and training programmes which are aimed at improving the quality of productive factors and making the UK more competitive on world markets. If successful, they will shift the aggregate supply curve to the right. Some economists have argued that it may be a good idea to encourage an increase in output, but it will not be very effective if there is not the additional demand to take up these extra products.
5/6 + 2/2 marks

e This is a good attempt at explaining how unemployment is measured and discussing the likely effectiveness of supply-side policies. The answer is well written and scores the maximum quality of written communication marks.

Scored 39/45 86.7% = Grade A

■ ■ ■

Response to question 3: grade C answer

(a) (i) Theoretically this is the total amount of products that can be produced by one country at one point in time. If a country has unemployed resources, then it is producing below its productive potential.
2/2 marks

(ii) An aggregate supply curve shows the total amount that can be produced in an economy and an aggregate demand curve the total amount that is being consumed.
0/2 marks

e This is a brief statement about what is meant by aggregate supply and demand. It does not deal with the curve.

(iii) Fiscal policy is how the government uses its budget. Monetary policy is how the government uses interest rates and money supply.
2/3 marks

e The candidate loses a mark because the answer is not fully explained.

(iv) This means that governments use the budget as a main tool of economic management most of the time and only use monetary policy occasionally.
0/3 marks

e The candidate misses the point that it is the relationship between fiscal and monetary policy which is being questioned.

(b) (i) They are consumer expenditure, investment, government expenditure and net expenditure on imports and exports.
4/4 marks

(ii) Aggregate demand curves are downward sloping from left to right because as product prices fall, so people can afford to buy more. This, of course, assumes that their income does not fall as well.
1/4 marks

e The candidate needs to develop the answer more fully (see grade A answer).

(iii) Disposable income is what is left in your pay after taxes and other things have been removed. The marginal propensity to consume is the proportion of each additional pound earned that you spend.
2/2 marks

(iv) If everyone's marginal propensity to consume goes up, then the aggregate demand curve shifts outwards, whereas it shifts inwards if their MPC goes down.
2/3 marks

 This answer is OK, but a fuller explanation is required for 3/3 marks.

(c) (i)

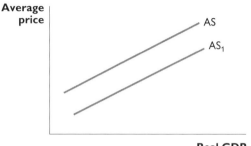

An outward shift in the supply curve from AS–AS$_1$ is an increase in the output of the economy which is not caused by a change in price. Economic growth in terms of an increase in the productive potential of an economy could have accounted for this.
2/6 marks

 The candidate seems to have dried up after writing about economic growth. An explanation of the various causes of economic growth — e.g. investment, invention and innovation — could have improved the mark.

(ii) The main injections into the circular flow are government expenditure, investment and exports. These are matched by the following leakages — taxation, saving and imports. If any of these change, they are likely to affect the aggregate demand curve first.
4/4 marks

(d) (ii) Economic growth is an increase in the productive capacity per person in an economy. When this occurs, it shifts the production possibility frontier outwards. For economic growth to be sustainable, non-renewable resources have to be replaced and/or recycled in the production process.

It is usual for people to expect that over their working life they will become better off and each successive generation hopes that it will be richer than the last. Governments also want to be able to do more to help the citizens of their country. All of these things can be achieved when an economy is growing.

However, growth can cause problems. There is an opportunity cost of investment which is a reduction in current consumption. There is a personal cost as a growing economy requires things to change and the workforce to be mobile. There are many frictions in the labour force which restrict occupational and geographical mobility.

question

Finally, growth carries external costs to society, such as pollution and congestion. Also, economic growth can lead to resources being used up more quickly and this may go against sustainability.

6/9 + 3/3 marks

A good answer which is well written. The costs are explained clearly, but the candidate does not incorporate evaluative comment in the answer.

Scored 28/45   62.2% = Grade C

Time allowed: 1 hour

Read the case study below. Answer parts (a) to (c). Choose either (d) (i) or (d) (ii) and write your answer in continuous prose. There are quality of written comminucation marks in (d) only.

Total marks allocated: 45.

The euro: to join or not to join?

Table 1 European interest, growth and inflation rates

	Interest rates (%)	Growth rates (%)	Inflation rates (%)
1998			
UK	7.4	2.6	2.3
France	3.6	3.2	0.6
Germany	3.5	1.8	0.9
Italy	4.8	1.5	2.0
Ireland	5.6	8.9	2.4
1999			
UK	5.4	2.1	2.1
France	2.9	2.9	0.5
Germany	2.9	1.4	0.6
Italy	2.9	1.4	1.7
Ireland	2.9	8.0	1.6

At the beginning of 1999, members of the EU — including France, Germany, Italy and Ireland — irrevocably fixed their currencies to the euro and agreed a date for the replacement of their domestic currencies by the euro. The UK postponed joining the single European currency and, since that time, the value of the pound sterling has appreciated against the euro. One of the main advantages of joining a single currency was a reduction in the costs of trading in many currencies and an increase in trade between those countries which are using the single unit of account. The main concern of the UK was the need for interest rates to converge, alongside the loss of control over monetary policy and exchange rate policy, plus the limits that would be imposed on the budget and fiscal policy.

(a) (i) **What is the difference between the RPI, RPIX and RPIY measures of inflation?** (3 marks)

(ii) **What was the real rate of interest in each country in 1998?** (2 marks)

(iii) **Use production possibility curves to illustrate the difference between growth in output and economic growth.** (3 marks)

(iv) **What is meant by 'the pound sterling has appreciated against the euro'?** (1 marks)

question

(b) (i) Explain and illustrate how interest rates are determined in a free market. (4 marks)
(ii) Explain how interest rates are determined in the **UK** and the **Eurozone**. (4 marks)
(iii) Looking at the interest rates for 1998 and 1999, explain why the **UK** may have been reluctant to join the euro in 1999. (4 marks)

(c) (i) Using the figures in Table 1, suggest whether the **UK** was right to think that joining the euro would raise its inflation rate and lower its growth rate. (4 marks)
(ii) Explain what is meant by the **UK** being concerned about 'the loss of control over monetary policy and exchange rate policy'. (4 marks)
(iii) Explain what is meant by the 'severe limits that would be imposed on the budget and fiscal policy'. (4 marks)

(d) **Either:**
(i) Discuss the effects on an economy of high accelerating inflation as opposed to low stable inflation. (12 marks)
or:
(ii) (a) Explain what is meant by the conflicts that occur in pursuit of the main macroeconomic policy objectives of government. (7 marks)
(b) Discuss whether fiscal and monetary policy can be used independently of each other to manage the economy. (5 marks)

Mark scheme

(a) (i) RPI is the retail price index measured as a weighted index including the prices of a selected basket of products (1 mark). RPIX does not include mortgage interest (1 mark). RPIY is RPIX minus local authority taxes and indirect taxes (1 mark).
(ii) Interest rate – inflation = real rate of interest, therefore UK = 5.1; France = 3.0; Germany = 2.6; Italy = 2.8; and Ireland = 3.2 (2 marks if all are correct, 1 mark if one or more are incorrect).
(iii) Diagram correctly labelled (1 mark), an explanation of a movement from inside the boundary towards the boundary (1 mark), shifting the boundary outwards (1 mark).
(iv) On foreign exchange markets, fewer pounds will be required to buy the same quantity of euros (1 mark).

(b) (i) Diagram correctly labelled (1 mark), explanation of demand for money and supply of money (3 marks). If a candidate uses loanable funds rather than liquidity preference theory, then allocate full marks.
(ii) Bank of England intervention in the UK (2 marks), European Central Bank (ECB) in Europe (2 marks).
(iii) Expect a recognition of relatively high rates in the UK compared with other countries and the low target set by the ECB (4 marks).

(c) (i) Growth rates and inflation rates both fell in the UK as they did for all the other countries, therefore there is no evidence to support the UK concern (4 marks).
(ii) Joining the euro fixes the pound against the euro and leaves the ECB to determine the rate with the rest of the world. Also, interest rates of 2.9% could be imposed on the UK (4 marks).

(iii) Given exchange rate and interest rate targets are set externally, the UK will have to be careful about the balance between taxation and expenditure, particularly in the case of a budget deficit (4 marks).

(d) Either:

(i) Expect a clear explanation of what is meant by 'high accelerating inflation' and 'low stable inflation'. On balance, the candidate should conclude that there are more disadvantages of a high accelerating rate of inflation due to:
- loss of purchasing power
- loss of confidence in the use of money
- indiscriminate redistributions of income and wealth
- loss of business confidence
- shoe leather and menu costs
- damaging effect on the exchange rate and interest rates

The candidate may see more advantages of low and stable inflation because this:
- avoids deflation
- stimulates the economy
- avoids falling nominal wages
- creates predictable borrowing rates and repayments
(9 marks + 3 marks for quality of written communication)

or:

(ii) (a) Explain how policies aimed at achieving any individual target set out below could aggravate the other targets of:
- low inflation
- high employment
- balance of payments equilibrium
- faster economic growth
(5 marks + 2 marks for quality of written communication)

(b) Expect some discussion of the effects that an expansionary fiscal policy can have on the money supply and interest rates, and how a contractionary monetary policy may impose a limit on the way in which a public sector borrowing requirement can be financed (4 marks + 1 mark for quality of written communication).

■ ■ ■

Response to question 4: grade A answer

(a) (i) The index of retail prices (RPI) is a weighted average of the index numbers that represent a selected basket of products. It shows the percentage rise or fall in prices. RPIX is the same figure excluding mortgage interest, and RPIY has the further exclusions of local authority taxes and indirect tax.
3/3 marks

(ii) In 1998, the real rate of interest in each country is the nominal rate minus the rate of inflation:
UK = 5.1%   ✓

question

France = 3.0%   ✓
Germany = 2.4%   ✗
Italy = 2.8%   ✓
Ireland = 3.2%   ✓
1/2 marks

e The candidate made a careless mistake with the German rate.

(iii)

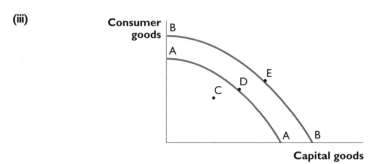

Economic growth is when the productive capacity of an economy increases. This shifts the boundary AA–BB. Therefore D–E is economic growth. If there are unemployed resources, then the economy can expand output from inside the boundary as illustrated by a move from C–D.
3/3 marks

(iv) The pound sterling appreciates in a floating exchange rate system when the price of sterling rises against the foreign currency. It means that the same pound will now buy more foreign currency.
1/1 marks

(b) (i)

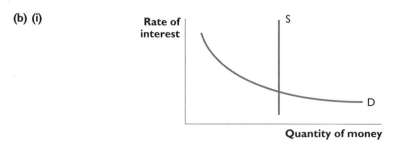

The supply of money is perfectly inelastic as it is exogenously determined by the Bank of England. The demand for money which is given its shape by the speculative demand, but also includes transactions and precautionary demand, is downward sloping from left to right. Where the two curves intersect is the equilibrium rate of interest.
4/4 marks

(ii) In the UK and the Eurozone, interest rates are not free to be determined by market forces, but the Bank of England and the European Central Bank intervene in the markets to set rates. They do this through the buying and selling of short-term government securities that maintain the required liquidity in the banking system and fix the agreed rate.

4/4 marks

(iii) In 1998, the interest rate in the UK was 7.4% while the average for the four Eurozone countries was 4.4%. In 1999, the UK rate was 5.4% and the Eurozone rate was 2.9%. It would therefore be the case that if the UK wanted to join the euro, it would have had to lower its interest rate to such an extent that many variables in the economy like borrowing, savings and investment would have been considerably disturbed.

4/4 marks

(c) (i) Between 1998 and 1999 the growth rate in the UK fell from 2.6% to 2.1%, which is a fall of 19.2%, while the average rate for the other countries fell by only 10.9%. Also, the inflation rate fell from 2.3% to 2.1%, which is a fall of 8.7%, while the average for the other countries was a fall of 25.4%. Without reference to any other evidence, it would seem that the UK was wrong because its growth rates were lower than the other countries and inflation rates were higher and fell less.

4/4 marks

(ii) If the UK joined the euro, then the ECB would gain control over UK monetary policy and exchange rate policy.

1/4 marks

There is only one relevant point in this answer. Otherwise it is a brief statement rather than an explanation.

(iii) The UK would not be able to do anything in its budget or in pursuit of fiscal control over the economy that would affect the monetary targets which are established by the European Central Bank.

3/4 marks

The candidate should have given more detail in the explanation.

(d) (i) A high accelerating rate of inflation would mean that the monthly rates would be rising and could reach what is termed hyperinflation where prices rise by hundreds and thousands of per cent per month. This type of inflation tends to damage the economy although a few people, such as those who own lots of real assets, may not be affected. Alternatively, a low and stable rate of inflation may have more benefits than costs to an economy.

A high rate of inflation brings about an indiscriminate redistribution of income and wealth. Those on fixed incomes become worse off while those who hold their assets in the form of money may see its value wiped out.

There are shoe leather costs of inflation as people hold minimum active money balances and are forever running to and from the bank. Also, there are menu costs of inflation as prices have to be changed regularly at the restaurant and

petrol pump. Another damaging effect of high inflation is the loss of business confidence that results from unstable prices, falling exchange rates and rising interest rates.

In contrast to the damage done by high rates of inflation, the existence of a low rate of inflation can be a positive benefit to an economy. It can stimulate demand in the economy and make business more buoyant. Business confidence is not damaged as interest rates and exchange rates will remain fairly stable.

Overall, although all types of inflation bring benefits to some and costs to others, there is probably a net benefit of a low and stable rate of inflation and a net cost to society of high accelerating inflation.

7/9 + 3/3 marks

Scored 38/45 84.4% = Grade A

■ ■ ■

Response to question 4: grade C answer

(a) (i) RPI stands for the retail price index, which is a weighted average index number that represents price changes in the economy. RPIX is the RPI minus mortgage repayments and RPIY is RPIX minus indirect taxes.

1/3 marks

e There are two small mistakes in this answer. First, it is mortgage interest payments, not repayments, and second, local taxes are missed in RPIY.

(ii) UK = 5.1%; France = 3.0%; Germany = 2.6%; Italy = 2.8%; Ireland = 3.2%.

1/2 marks

e The candidate gets the right answer, but does not state what is meant by the real rate of interest and therefore loses 1 mark.

(iii) Growth in an economy can occur when unemployed resources are used and the economy moves closer to its full productive potential.

1/3 marks

e A good explanation of growth in output, but it loses 2 marks for not including a diagram and an explanation of economic growth.

(iv) If the pound sterling has appreciated, this means that more pounds will have to be used to buy the same amount of foreign currency.

0/1 mark

e This answer is the wrong way round — the candidate describes depreciation.

(b) (i) In a free market the rate of interest is said to be determined either by the interaction of the supply and demand for money or by the interaction of the supply of savings and the demand for loans.

Either

Or

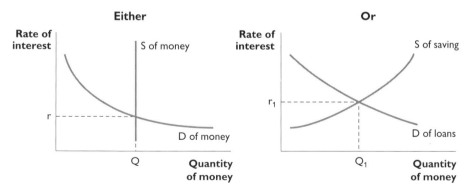

As the rate of interest falls, so the speculative demand for money rises and the demand for loans increases. Meanwhile, the supply of savings falls and the supply of money remains unchanged.
4/4 marks

(ii) In the UK and Eurozone, interest rates are determined by market forces but with some government intervention either on the demand or supply side to establish a rate that is consistent with the policy of the UK government or the European Union. At present, the UK rate is higher than the Eurozone rate, as illustrated by the figures for 1999, i.e. 5.4% and 2.9%.
4/4 marks

(iii) Interest rates in the UK are much higher than those in the other countries of Europe.
1/4 marks

🖉 The statement is correct, but there is no explanation of the point.

(c) (i) Looking at the statistics in Table 1, there is no evidence that the rate of inflation has increased in any of the countries that are part of the euro. The growth rate, however, has fallen in all the Eurozone countries, but the fact that it has fallen even more in the UK does not suggest that belonging to the euro was the problem.
3/4 marks

🖉 Although this answer is correct, the candidate needs to make a more precise reference to the statistics in Table 1.

(ii) If the UK joined the single European currency, the European Bank would determine the level of interest rates as well as influencing the exchange rate of the euro against the rest of the world's currencies. Also, there would be no exchange rate between Eurozone countries, therefore it would not be possible to adjust the pound against the franc or the mark.
4/4 marks

(iii) Not being able to change interest rates will limit the opportunity to stimulate aggregate demand.
2/4 marks

🖉 This answer is correct as far as it goes, but not relevant to answering the question.

(d) (ii) (a) The government has four main macroeconomic policy objectives. They are to maintain a high level of employment, a low stable rate of inflation, a satisfactory balance of payments, and a growing economy. What is meant by the question is that pursuit of any one of these policy objectives may have a damaging effect on another policy target.

If the government tried to raise aggregate demand to increase employment, it may also encourage growth, but cause the rate of inflation to rise and the current balance on the balance of payments to move into deficit.

If the government tried to reduce inflation by reducing aggregate demand, then this may benefit the external account, but worsen the chances of economic growth and cause unemployment to rise.

3/5 + 2/2 marks

(b) Yes, fiscal policy can be used independently from monetary policy. Fiscal policy is how the government affects aggregate demand by changing the balance between revenue from taxation and government expenditure. A budget deficit means that expenditure exceeds taxation and is therefore expansionary, while a budget surplus can be used to dampen down demand.

Monetary policy is concerned with the ways that the government can expand the economy by increasing the money supply and/or reducing interest rates.

2/4 + 1/1 marks

The quality of written communication in this answer is good and achieves maximum marks, but in part (a) some marks were lost for not fully developing the answer. In part (b) the candidate has not responded to the word 'discuss' in the question. The explanation of how fiscal and monetary policy are used is correct, but there is no indication that the candidate is aware of the impact that a change in, say, fiscal policy could have on monetary policy and vice versa.

Scored 29/45 64.4% = Grade C

Time allowed: 1 hour

Read the case study below. Answer parts (a) to (c). Choose either (d)(i) or (d)(ii) and write your answer in continuous prose. There are quality of written communication marks in (d) only.

Total marks allocated: 45.

The UK economy in and out of the single European currency

Table 1 The single European currency

1998	Actual		Forecast – euro		Forecast + euro	
	1998	**1999**	**2000**	**2001**	**2000**	**2001**
Interest rate (%)	7.4	5.4	6.1	6.5	2.9	3.4
Growth (%)	2.6	2.1	3.0	2.3	3.1	3.5
Inflation (%)	2.3	2.1	2.1	2.5	2.8	3.1
Unemployment (m)	1.31	1.25	1.10	1.15	1.05	1.00
Current account balance (£m)	–655	–12,761	–17,000	–15,000	–19,000	–17,000
£M4 (%)	3.8	5.0	4.9	5.0	5.9	7.0
Euro-£ rate	1.50	1.52	1.66	1.72	1.52	1.52
Euro-$ rate	0.90	0.93	1.19	1.22	1.19	1.22

Joan Cuthbertson, a little-known but well respected economist, developed her own economic model for producing economic forecasts. Over the last 10 years, she has out-performed the Treasury model and more interest has been shown in her forecasts.

At the end of 1999, Cuthbertson produced two forecasts for the key UK economic variables in the years 2000 and 2001. The first pair (forecast – euro) were based upon the assumption that the UK did not join the single European currency, while the second pair (forecast + euro) were based upon the assumption that the UK joined the European currency at the beginning of 2000.

For the UK economy, it was predicted that joining the euro would lower unemployment, increase inflation and the growth of £M4 as well as increasing the current balance deficit. Cuthbertson had stated that if the UK joined the single European currency, then the government must place much greater emphasis on the use of supply-side policies to manage the overall level of economic activity.

(a) Using figures from Table 1, explain what is meant by and what happened to the following economic variables between 1998 and 1999.
  (i) current account balance (3 marks)

5

question

    (ii) £M4   (3 marks)

    (iii) euro-dollar rate   (3 marks)

(b) (i) There is a significant difference between the forecast for interest rates if the UK joins or does not join the euro. Choose three of the economic variables listed in Table 1 and explain how the different predictions may be related to the different forecasts for interest rates.   (9 marks)

    (ii) If the UK joined the single European currency, which two economic variables listed in Table 1 would the European Central Bank have most control over?   (2 marks)

(c) (i) What is meant by the statement 'if the UK joined the single European currency, then the government must place much greater emphasis on the use of supply-side policies to manage the overall level of economic activity'?   (6 marks)

    (ii) If the UK joined the euro then, with reference to the euro-dollar rate, describe the likely impact on its trade with the US.   (3 marks)

    (iii) The years 2000 and 2001 are forecasts. Offer one reason why forecasts vary significantly and one other reason why the actual outcome may be significantly different from the forecast.   (4 marks)

(d) Either:

    (i) Discuss the ways in which the level of unemployment can be reduced and suggest which solution is least likely to aggravate inflation.   (12 marks)

    or:

    (ii) Explain how monetary policy can be used to manage the economy and suggest how effective it is likely to be.   (12 marks)

Mark scheme

(a) (i) Definition of current account balance (2 marks), correct description of change (1 mark).

    (ii) Definition of £M4 (2 marks), correct description of change (1 mark).

    (iii) Correct description of euro-dollar rate (2 marks), correct description of change (1 mark).

(b) (i) Three of the listed economic variables explained in relation to the interest rate differentials (3 × 3 marks).

    (ii) Two from interest rate, £M4, euro-£ rate (2 marks).

(c) (i) Explain the loss of control over monetary policy (2 marks), explain less control over fiscal policy (2 marks), explain the use of supply-side policies (2 marks).

    (ii) In 2000 and 2001 recognise that the value of the UK currency will be lower and therefore export prices will be lower and import prices higher. This will impact on the current account balance (3 marks).

    (iii) Forecasts vary because of different assumptions (2 marks) and are not usually correct as an economy is dynamic and things change over time (2 marks).

(d) Either:

    (i) Expect an explanation and discussion of the various demand-side policies including monetary, fiscal and exchange rate, and supply-side policies including attempts to increase market freedom, improve incentives and promote developments in productivity, followed by a conclusion that supply-side policies are least likely to aggravate inflation (9 marks + 3 marks for quality of written communication).

or:

(ii) An explanation of monetary policy and how it is used (4 marks) and some evaluative comment about its effectiveness (5 marks) plus 3 marks for quality of written communication.

■ ■ ■

Response to question 5: grade A answer

(a) (i) The current account balance of the balance of payments is the difference between the total value of exported goods and services and imported goods and services over a given period of time. Between 1998 and 1999 the value of imports rose relative to the value of exports such that the deficit grew from –£655m to –£12,761m.
3/3 marks

(ii) This refers to the M4 definition of money in the UK. It is a broad money measure which includes cash and chequeable accounts plus other forms of near money such as deposit accounts at banks and building societies. Between 1998 and 1999 this broad money aggregate grew faster, rising from 3.8% in 1998 to 5% in 1999.
3/3 marks

✎ Full marks are allocated as the candidate understands the main components of broad money even though precise detail — like the inclusion of certificates of deposit — is omitted.

(iii) The euro to dollar exchange rate shows how many euros it takes to buy one dollar on the foreign currency market. This rate may change from minute to minute as the euro currency floats against the US$. In 1998, 0.9 of a euro was required to buy one dollar, and in 1999, 0.93 was required. This means that the value of the euro has depreciated against the dollar.
3/3 marks

(b) (i) Given lower interest rates, the rate of economic growth is projected to be higher. This is because lower rates will boost investment which is one of the main causes of economic growth. As the economy grows faster, so the level of unemployment is likely to fall which is why the forecast + euro shows lower levels of unemployment. However, faster rates of growth in the economy are likely to increase demand for imported components and raw materials and this is why the forecast current account balance is estimated to produce an even larger deficit if the UK joins the euro.
6/9 marks

✎ Good points are made, but not always fully explained and — given the chosen economic variables — nothing is said about the effect on aggregate demand of lower interest rates. Each variable is analysed from the supply side.

(ii) Interest rates and money supply, which together make up monetary policy.
2/2 marks

(c) (i) As described above, the main components of monetary demand — namely the rate of interest and money supply — come under the umbrella of the European Central Bank. As the UK loses control over these variables, this will impose a significant limitation on the government's scope to use fiscal policy to stimulate or contract aggregate demand. This means that the best way to deal with imbalances between aggregate supply and aggregate demand will be to control the supply side of the economy, e.g. adjustments to tax rates to motivate workers and firms or improved education and training to increase labour productivity.
6/6 marks

(ii) The euro/dollar rate and therefore the euro/pound rate is much lower if the UK is in the single European currency. The result of this in terms of the flow of trade with the US is that exports will be cheaper and imports will be more expensive. The final effect that this will have upon the balance of payments depends upon the demand elasticity for imports and exports.
3/3 marks

(iii) Forecasts may vary significantly as different forecasters will make different assumptions and include different variables.
2/4 marks

e Half marks because the answer only deals with the forecast and does not look at the outcome.

(d) (ii) Suppose it was necessary to use monetary policy to expand aggregate monetary demand. Basically there are two ways of expanding monetary demand.

Firstly, the Monetary Policy Committee of the Bank of England can decide to lower interest rates. This can have two expansionary effects. It can encourage more investment in capital, as it becomes more profitable for firms to borrow and expand their productive capacity, or it can encourage consumers to increase their borrowing, particularly to purchase higher priced consumer durables. However, neither of these things are guaranteed to take place if interest rates are lowered.

The second approach is directly to expand the money supply to boost government expenditure and in this case a part of the public sector borrowing requirement will be financed by printing money. While this technique boosts demand, it may also have damaging effects on the rate of inflation in the economy. If it is considered necessary to contract monetary demand, then interest rates can be raised and over-funding can remove money from circulation.

Either approach may not have the desired effect as it could be that inflation and exchange rates may be adversely affected. For example, an attempt to boost aggregate monetary demand may cause more imports to be demanded and potential exports to be sold off in the domestic market, leading to a deterioration in the balance of payments.

7/9 + 3/3 marks

e A well written and good attempt at trying to evaluate the effectiveness of monetary policy.

Scored 38/45   84.4% = Grade A

■ ■ ■

Response to question 5: grade C answer

(a) (i) The current account balance refers to the government's budget. In 1998 it had a deficit of –£655m which by 1999 grew to –£12,761m.

0/3 marks

e This answer confuses the government budget with the required component of the balance of payments.

(ii) M4 is a measurement of the UK money supply that includes notes, coins and bank balances, some of which can be immediately accessed by cheque and others that are savings accounts.

2/3 marks

e The candidate scores 2 on the description, but fails to refer to the figures in Table 1 as the question asks.

(iii) The euro-dollar rate is the exchange rate between the European Union and the US. In 1998, 0.9 of a euro was required to buy a dollar. By 1999, the euro had appreciated to 0.93 of a euro to the dollar.

2/3 marks

e The candidate loses a mark because the description is of a depreciation in the value of the euro, rather than the appreciation as stated in the answer.

(b) (i) Outside the euro, interest rates are predicted to be 6.1% and 6.5% respectively. If the UK had joined the single currency, the estimates for the same years would be much lower at 2.9% and 3.4%. The lower interest rates would have encouraged more borrowing and the money supply has grown faster at 5.9% and 7% compared with 4.9% and 5% with higher rates. Along with this higher estimated growth in money supply is a slightly higher inflation rate at 2.8% and 3.1% instead of 2.1% and 2.5%. Altogether this higher level of aggregate demand has produced a small acceleration in the economic growth rate which is estimated to be at 2.8% and 3.1% compared with the deceleration from 3.0% to 2.5%.

7/9 marks

e A good use of the figures, though slightly more explanation would be required for full marks.

(ii) Interest rate.
1/2 marks

✎ This answer needs to include exchange rate.

(c) (i) There are broadly four main ways that the government can control the overall level of economic activity. They are fiscal policy, monetary policy, exchange rate policy and supply-side policy. The first three would be controlled from the centre of Europe with the UK government only being able to make adjustments to the various components that make up aggregate supply, such as the motivations of entrepreneurs and the workforce.
4/6 marks

✎ There is more flexibility in the use of fiscal policy than is suggested in this answer. A little more explanation is required.

(ii) The value of the euro is higher and, if the UK joined the euro, then it would be more difficult to sell exports to the US as they would be more expensive, but easier for the US to sell to the UK as their exports would be cheaper.
0/3 marks

✎ The candidate makes the same mistake, and misreads statistics which indicate a depreciation in the value of the euro relative to the dollar, not an appreciation.

(iii) Forecasts vary significantly from one another because the assumptions made when the models are constructed vary from forecaster to forecaster. Also the economy is dynamic and between the time the forecast is made and the actual event taking place there may be unexpected changes.
4/4 marks

(d) (i) The level of unemployment can be unacceptably high. For example, in the past unemployment has been as high as nearly one quarter of the workforce or as low as 2%. Facing this considerable difference, governments have taken it upon themselves to try and manage the economy to a stable high level of employment.

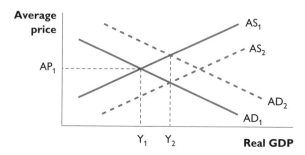

In the diagram above we can assume that Y_1 is the current equilibrium level of employment, but Y_2 has been achievable in the past and may be achievable now. Given this information, there are two ways to move from Y_1 to Y_2. Either the aggregate demand curve can be shifted to the right by expansionary fiscal and/or monetary policies, or the lowering of the exchange rate, or the aggregate supply curve could be shifted to the right using supply-side policies. It is these supply-side policies that are least likely to aggravate inflation.

6/9 + 3/3 marks

A well-constructed and well-written answer with all the main points included. However, there is not sufficient detail to achieve a higher mark. For example, fiscal and monetary policy are referred to, but neither are explained.

Scored 29/45   64.4% = Grade C

Time allowed: 1 hour

Read the case study below. Answer parts (a) to (c). Choose either (d) (i) or (d) (ii) and write your answer in continuous prose. There are quality of written communication marks in (d) only.

Total marks allocated: 45.

Changing expenditure patterns

The statistics in Table 1 below indicate that since 1996 there have been significant changes in the components of expenditure that make up the UK's gross domestic product. The government has tried, in its expenditure plans, to avoid crowding out the private sector and recognised the importance of the multiplier effect on investment in the economy. There is evidence that more is being produced to be shared among a relatively static total population.

Table 1 Expenditure and the gross domestic product (constant prices, 1995 £m)

	Consumer spending	Government spending	Investment	Exports	Imports	GDP	Population size (M)	GDP/ capita
1996	470,622	142,820	123,686	217,600	223,961		58.6	
1997	488,936	140,824	135,322	236,283	244,635		58.7	
1998	504,518	141,810	149,704	241,696	266,164		59.1	
1999	524,228	147,982	152,014	249,093	286,273		59.1	

(a) (i) **Define GDP and calculate the figures that should appear in the columns for GDP and GDP per capita in Table 1.** (4 marks)

   (ii) **Which component of GDP showed the largest percentage change between 1996 and 1999?** (1 mark)

  (iii) **What are the three ways of measuring GDP? Identify one problem associated with each measurement.** (6 marks)

  (iv) **The statistics in Table 1 are measured at 'constant prices 1995'. What does this mean and, therefore, what changes are being illustrated in the table?** (3 marks)

(b) (i) **Which component of GDP is likely to accelerate the rate of economic growth? Explain your choice.** (3 marks)

  (ii) **Identify the percentage change in 'government spending' and 'investment' for the periods 1996–98 and 1998–99.** (2 marks)

  (iii) **What is 'crowding out'? Explain how the answer to (b) (ii) could be an example of crowding out.** (4 marks)

(c) (i) **Between 1996 and 1999, compare the overall change in 'consumer spending' with that of 'investment'.** (2 marks)

(ii) **What are the main determinants of:**
  - **consumer spending**
  - **investment** (4 marks)

(iii) **'Changes in investment have a multiplier effect on GDP.' What does this statement mean?** (4 marks)

(d) **Either:**
  (i) **Evaluate the advantages and disadvantages to an economy of having a high proportion of its GDP determined by the flow of imports and exports.** (12 marks)
  or:
  (ii) **Discuss whether there should be more or less government intervention in the macroeconomic management of the economy.** (12 marks)

Mark scheme

(a) (i) Expect a definition in terms of expenditure income or output (2 marks). For a correct set of GDP figures (1 mark) and GDP per capita (1 mark).

	GDP	GDP/capita
1996	730,767	12,470
1997	756,730	12,891
1998	771,564	13,055
1999	787,044	13,317

(ii) Investment + 22.9% (1 mark).

(iii) Income (1 mark), output (1 mark), expenditure (1 mark), plus one example of a problem for each, e.g. self-provided products (income) (1 mark), double counting (output) (1 mark), changes in the value of money (expenditure) (1 mark).

(iv) All components of GDP are measured as if the prices are fixed at the 1995 level (1 mark). This removes any distortion caused by changes in the value of money (1 mark) and therefore shows changes in output or real GDP (1 mark).

(b) (i) It is most likely that investment (1 mark) will be chosen, although a reasoned case can be made for other variables. An explanation of the relationship between investment and economic growth (2 marks).

(ii) Government spending, –0.7% and 4.4% (1 mark); investment, 21% and 1.5% (1 mark).

(iii) Explain crowding out (2 marks) and explain how when government spending falls, investment rises but when government expenditure rises, investment slows down (2 marks).

(c) (i) Consumer spending rose by 11.4% whereas investment rose more than twice as fast at 22.9% (2 marks).

(ii) Expect at least a sentence to explain the determinants of consumer spending to include things such as disposable income, level and rate of change of income, attitude towards saving and spending, distribution of income, structure of population, interest rates etc. (2 marks), and for investment expect things such as interest rates, business

confidence, expectations, government policy, marginal efficiency of investment etc. (2 marks).

(iii) Expect reference to investment being an injection into the circular flow of income and a description of how an injection of a certain amount will bring about successive rises in income such that the final change in income is greater than the initial change (4 marks).

(d) Either:

(i) The answer should pass a critical eye over the advantages of a high proportion of international trade, including greater variety, more efficient allocation of resources, higher real incomes, greater interdependence. For disadvantages the answer should include dependency on foreign traders, significant risk of dumping, less stable exchange rate, strategic problems, disruption to supply etc. (9 marks + 3 marks for quality of written communication).

or:

(ii) There are various ways of answering this question. For example, a candidate may take each of the macroeconomic problems and evaluate the degree to which more or less involvement may produce benefits. Alternatively, a comparison of the views regarding the weaknesses of capitalism and the need for governments to compensate in the form of demand management, or a recognition of the strengths of capitalism and the need for governments to withdraw from active management and encourage free markets and competition (9 marks + 3 marks for quality of written communication).

■ ■ ■

Response to question 6: grade A answer

(a) (i) GDP is gross domestic product which is a measure of how much is produced in an economy over a given period of time. The GDP figures are calculated from the equation GDP = C + G + I + X − M. Therefore:

1996 = 730,767
1997 = 756,730
1998 = 771,564
1999 = 787,044

The GDP per capita is GDP divided by the total population:

1996 = 12,470
1997 = 12,891
1998 = 13,055
1999 = 13,317

4/4 marks

(ii) Investment changes the most, increasing by 22.9%.

1/1 mark

(iii) The economy can be measured by adding up all the expenditure over a period of time and, where inflation is a problem, this needs to be removed in order to identify real changes. Alternatively, the output of all the firms can be added together. To avoid double counting, it is necessary to measure only the value added by each firm. The final measure is to add up everyone's income, while recognising the problem that people do not always provide correct information about their income.

6/6 marks

(iv) The product of the economy is measured as if prices never change from the 1995 figures. The result of this is that the figures show real changes in output rather than nominal changes in the value of money.

3/3 marks

(b) (i) Investment is the purchase of capital in the form of new machines and factories. Increases in this area of expenditure are likely to boost the productive potential of the economy.

3/3 marks

(ii) Government spending fell by –0.7% and then rose by 4.4% while investment rose by 21% followed by 1.5%.

2/2 marks

(iii) Crowding out is when government spending — particularly when financed by public sector borrowing and higher interest rates — restricts private investment and consumption. In the figures identified above there is a considerable rise in investment, i.e. 21%, when government expenditure falls, but a much smaller rise of only 1.5% when government spending rises 4.4% in 1 year.

4/4 marks

(c) (i) Investment rose by 22.9% which is slightly more than twice the rise in consumer spending, which grew by 11.4%.

2/2 marks

(ii) The level of consumer spending in the economy depends upon the rate of interest. Lower rates encourage more borrowing. Also the level of a person's income affects their spending pattern. Arguably, higher income leads to more spending, though the marginal propensity to consume may fall at higher levels of income. Investment is determined by the rate of interest and the marginal efficiency of capital investment, i.e. the return on capital.

2/4 marks

The answer only deals with two points for consumer spending and two for investment.

(iii) Investment is an injection into the circular flow of income. Because income is created through the process of derived demand, then the total effect on income will be greater than the original change in investment.

3/4 marks

This answer is a little too brief for full marks.

(d) (i) If a high proportion of GDP is determined by international trade and this trade is due to free trade without barriers, then economic theory tells us that absolute advantage and comparative advantage will produce gains from trade. This is likely to mean that standards of living will be higher than if a country had little international trade because of protective barriers. The high level of free international trade should produce a more efficient allocation of resources and higher real incomes.

A greater exposure to international trade increases the variety of products available to the consumer. Also, the increased competition between firms worldwide drives prices down and improves the quality of products on the market.

In contrast, a high dependency on imports can make a country vulnerable to things outside its control. For example, one country may be able to threaten another country at a diplomatic level or even talk about war if it has control of supply over a vital resource like food.

Depency on foreign firms may also damage a firm or whole industry if supply of important raw materials or components is interrupted by strike action which is outside the control of the domestic economy. Similarly, political decisions may be made in one country that significantly affect the flow of imports and exports to the host country. This may deprive consumers of the choice they previously had.
7/9 + 3/3 marks

e A well-written answer with a good range of points, but there could have been a little more evaluation. For example, it is desirable to draw the threads of argument together in a conclusion.

Scored 40/45 88.9% = Grade A

■ ■ ■

Response to question 6: grade C answer

(a) (i) GDP is C + G + I + X − M.
1996 = 730,767; 1997 = 756,730; 1998 = 771,564; and 1999 = 787,044.
GDP per capita is per person, therefore:
1996 = 12,470; 1997 = 12,891; 1998 = 13,055; and 1999 = 13,317.
3/4 marks

e The answer needs to include a little more detail on GDP, i.e. a measure of domestic output over a period of time.

(ii) Consumer spending rises by £53,606 from £470,622 to £524,228.
0/1 marks

e The question asks for the largest percentage change.

(iii) The three ways of measuring GDP are income, output and expenditure, and three problems are difficulties of collecting statistics, the black market (where unrecorded transactions take place) and inflation.
5/6 marks

e The candidate loses 1 mark for not relating the problems identified to a particular measure, as the question asks.

(iv) Constant prices mean the prices that existed in 1995 and therefore the statistics do not include inflation.
2/3 marks

e This answer is almost there, but in order to get the third mark the candidate should have made a reference to 'real' or 'output'.

(b) (i) A rise in exports injects spending into the circular flow of income and this in turn boosts aggregate demand and stimulates economic growth.
2/3 marks

e The candidate did not choose investment, but makes out a reasonable case for exports. However, the impact of exports is more likely to be on growth in output than a growth in productive potential.

(ii) Between 1996 and 1998 government spending falls by a few percent and investment rises a lot. However, between 1998 and 1999 the government expenditure rises a lot more than investment.
0/2 marks

e The candidate is asked for percentages and seems not to know how to calculate them.

(iii) Crowding out is where the public sector interferes in the private sector of the economy. Crowding out could have happened between 1998 and 1999 because the government was spending a lot more money.
0/4 marks

e Uninspired guesswork.

(c) (i) The overall change in consumer spending was a rise of £53,606m, while the increase in investment was only £28,328m. This means that consumer spending has grown twice as fast as investment.
0/2 marks

e The candidate has not realised that the comparative change is the other way round if one looks at the rate of change rather than the raw totals, i.e. investment is growing at twice the rate of consumer spending.

(ii) The main determinants of consumer spending are the consumers' income, their attitude to spending and saving and how much money they can borrow at a specific interest rate. The main determinants of investment are again the rate of interest, how fast the economy is growing and how profitable a new investment may be in the future.
4/4 marks

(iii) When a government decides to invest in a new motorway, lots of people will be employed and paid an income. They in turn will go to the shops and spend their

question

income on food and drink etc. With the money they spend in the shops, the shopkeeper can go out and buy more things and so it goes on. This means that the final effect on everyone's income is much greater than the original amount of money invested in producing the new motorway, and GDP rises by a multiple of the original change.

4/4 marks

e A simplistic — but correct — description of how the multiplier works.

(d) (ii) Governments intervene in the economy to manage the macroeconomic problems of high unemployment, high inflation, balance of payment disequilibrium and low or no economic growth.

In the past, the main thrust of macroeconomic management was to use fiscal policies, monetary policies and exchange rate policies to manipulate aggregate demand. This fine tuning is aimed at stabilising the economy at a full employment equilibrium. The pursuit of this type of demand-side policy was a recognition that capitalism had weak self-regulatory mechanisms and could settle at high levels of unemployment over sustained periods of time.

For a period of time after the Second World War these policies seemed to be successful, but in the seventies and eighties it became obvious that governments were not able to reconcile the big economic problems.

Over recent years, there has been a different approach to economic management which has meant less intervention by government. Government no longer talks about full employment targets and has made an independent Bank of England responsible for achieving an inflation target. It seems that government has recognised the benefits of not interfering in a market economy and many state-run industries have been returned to the private sector. Government has been most concerned to encourage competition and to motivate workers and firms into becoming more productive.

There are strong opinions on both sides of this argument, but it does seem that at this point in time the argument for less government intervention is in the ascendancy.

8/9 + 3/3 marks

e A well-written answer with some attempt at a conclusion.

Scored 31/45 68.9% = Grade C